D0835772

The Winchester Story

Barry Shurlock

MILESTONE PUBLICATIONS ®

Acknowledgements

The major published sources used in the research for this short book are given above under Further Reading. The *Winchester Studies* produced under the aegis of the Winchester Research Unit and published by Oxford University Press, further volumes of which are in preparation (see Biddle, 1984), are particularly recommended to the serious reader.

Many of the pictures were taken especially for this publication, while others are published with the permission of the individuals and bodies credited in the captions. Thanks for help with obtaining pictures are also due to John Hardacre, Cathedral Curator; George Walsh of the *Hampshire Chronicle*; Philippa Stevens, Winchester Local Studies Librarian; James Sabben-Clare, Headmaster of Winchester College; Karen Parker of the Winchester City Museums; Jean Wright of The Printed Page, Winchester; Alan Bates, Manager of the Domesday 900 Exhibition; John Phipps, The Courts Administrator; and David Witcher of the University of Southampton Teaching Media.

Many of the photographic prints were produced by John King or Derek Dine.

The drawing of Winchester Castle (Figure 14) was first published in *Winchester Castle and The Great Hall* by Martin Biddle and Beatrice Clayre, published by the Hampshire County Council.

B.S.

©1986 Barry Shurlock

Published by Milestone Publications,
62 Murray Road, Horndean, Hampshire PO8 9JL

British Library Cataloguing in Publication Date

Shurlock, Barry
  The Winchester story.
  1. Winchester (Hampshire)——History
  I. Title
  942.2'735   DA690.W67

  ISBN 0-903852-91-8

Phototypeset by Monitor Publications Ltd, Hayling Island

Printed and bound in Great Britain by
R.J. Acford, Chichester, W. Sussex

Contents

The south side of Winchester Cathedral seen through one of the arches of the former chapter house of St Swithun's Priory

A City of Treasures

'As for myself, I am always rewarded for any amount of trouble in going to Winchester'
— Sir Walter Besant

The Portsmouth-born novelist who wrote these words had just shown some friends what he called 'this wonderful treasury of things ancient and lovely'.

If he were to come to Winchester again today he would still see most of the same sights that thrilled him almost a century ago, albeit in a better state of preservation: the cathedral, St. Cross Hospital, the Great Hall and Round Table, Winchester College, the City Cross, Godbegot House and many other 'treasures'.

There would of course be some new sights, such as the imposing bronze statue of King Alfred at the east end of the city, which Besant himself advocated. But the Hampshire writer would probably be most impressed by the vast amount of 'new history' that has come from excavation and re-examination of old documents.

In particular, over the past twenty-five years the activities of Professor Martin Biddle and the Winchester Research Unit, founded in 1968, have transformed the story of the city's past. The vast treasure-house of information that for centuries has been under the ground or in specialised libraries has been revealed and reinterpreted. And the work continues: some of its fruits can be seen in the City Museum.

The Winchester story has also been researched by many others, in particular Mrs Barbara Carpenter Turner, twice mayor, who was dubbed 'the Winchester-in-General expert' by the late Sir Nikolaus Pevsner.

For visitor and resident alike this modern explosion of antiquarian activity means that much of the 'old history' needs revision if the story of Winchester is to be told properly. This is particularly true for the Saxon period, when Winchester was the principal city in the south, the first capital of the emerging state of England.

At the centre of the Saxon city was the Old Minster, which stood to the north of the existing Norman cathedral. Archaeologists have in recent years uncovered the foundations of this great church and the fruits of their labours are outlined on the turf for visitors to see.

The story of Winchester during the Middle Ages must also take account of the publication of a vast amount of new information in the volumes of the *Winchester Studies.*.

The complex stories of Winchester Castle, the Round Table and the King's House have also been investigated anew to yield a better understanding of a site where royal, civic and military power has been exercised for more than 900 years.

Most recently, the Domesday 900 Exhibition has brought together recent work on the great 'inventory' prepared in Winchester for William the Conqueror twenty years after the Conquest. Winchester itself was excluded, though later surveys, collectively known as The Winton Domesday, provide the same sort of detailed picture of life under the Normans.

In this short publication I have tried to retell some parts of *The Winchester Story* in the light of modern studies. It is a celebration of a city I have lived in for more than a decade and a personal tribute to those who have studied it. I would be astonished if individual experts did not find something to dispute, though I have tried to take account of the most recent sources and hope that readers will be encouraged to consult them for more details.

The individual stories which make up the book have been chosen to illustrate the major events in the city's past and have been arranged with some chronological sense. Readers new to the city are advised to consult the brief chronology and list of 'Winchester words' at the back.

Winchester is a small city and an ideal place to explore on foot. Its compactness emphasises the close relationships between secular and religious power, art and religion and learning and religion that have shaped the English world.

'Hills', Where It Began

'It seems impossible that sixty years can have passed since I stood on the bank of the circumvallation facing towards Winchester and gazed down at the white morning mist that entirely concealed the city and valley.'

— T.A. Trollope, 1886

According to tradition, Winchester is said to have started on St Catherine's Hill, the prominent down which gazes down on walkers strolling beside the River Itchen below the city.

It is an enchanting spot with an unbeatable view of the city and the valley below, particularly at night or in the early morning. It is ideal for a jaunt, a bit of madness, a revel, a celebration, a distant gaze.

The hill has always been a popular destination for walkers, who today make their way up from a path which starts at the east end of Garnier Road. Passing close by Plague Pits Valley, where the unfortunate victims of disease were once buried, they aim for a ring of beech trees at the top. These were originally planted by the Militia in 1762 and contain the foundations of St Catherine's Chapel, a medieval church destroyed after the Reformation.

Around the summit of the hill runs a deep and impressive ditch which was excavated between the wars and dated to the Iron Age. Like many other hill fortifications in the south, it seems to have been suddenly stormed and abandoned, in this case around 150 BC or earlier.

Although the very first 'Winchester' is often identified with the hill, elsewhere in the city in the vicinity of Oram's Arbour is a huge Iron Age site, which is comparable with such forts as Maiden Castle in Dorset. It is partly covered by the north-west corner of the later walled town that was built by the Romans, and it may have extended to Jewry Street or beyond.

(Oddly, the name Old Winchester Hill belongs to another, larger hill fort which stands on the east bank of the Meon above Warnford, twelve miles away, but seems to have nothing whatever to do with the city.)

A few miles to the west of Winchester, near Stockbridge, is yet another similar fort, Danebury, which has been excavated in recent years by the archaeologist Professor Barry Cunliffe. His work suggests that this fort was very much a community of its own, a sort of kraal township controlling its neighbourhood and offering the fruits of trade and a wide range of crafts.

Perhaps St Catherine's Hill was similar. Certainly it is in an imposing position, standing above the relatively narrow valley of the River Itchen and an easy day's march from the coast. It would therefore have stood between any invader and the hinterland. On a clear day the Solent can readily be seen from another of the locality's beauty spots, Cheesefoot Head, three miles to the east.

St Catherine's Hill was a relatively large fort, with more than a thousand yards of ditch, which led the famous antiquarian, General Pitt-Rivers, to suggest that more than three thousand men would have been needed for its defence.

Until the early 19th century a beacon stood on the hill, ready to be lit in case of an invasion. The lonely task of the old watchman, waiting for signals from the South Coast, was no doubt relieved by ragging of the boys from Winchester College, for specific instructions were issued 'not to allow them into the hut or to pull straw off the beacon'.

The tradition of college boys using the hill as a playground goes back at least until the middle of the 16th century. At the start and end of each day they trooped up in double file 'whipped in' by prefects and were then left to do more or less what they wanted.

As well as smoking and drinking, their high-jinks included 'chariot races', 'mouse-digging', badger hunts and other more dignified studies of natural history. Called 'Hills' by the boys, this ritual provided an ideal opportunity to get some exercise and burn up boyish energy.

One former Wykehamist writing fifty years ago recorded his memories of Hills: 'East and west and south there was open country close at hand; water-meadows with their glittering streams, downs on either hand. . . Had any other school a country so alluring to a boy who loved the open air?'

That unique sport Winchester Football, the college's equivalent of the Eton Wall Game, is said to have been first played on the hill. It originally involved long lines of boys along each side of the pitch to prevent the ball from being lost down the slope, though modern versions of the game achieve the same end with the aid of nets.

One gruesome tradition about St Catherine's Hill is said to explain the origins of an ancient maze which can be found on its summit and is still walkable. It runs between low grass banks to the centre of the area and is a simple maze with no dead-ends. Yet it has been cunningly cut so that the goal seems to be in sight just as the path sweeps away

St Catherine's Hill from the Itchen Navigation below Wharf Bridge

on some new twist!

According to the tale, the mismaze, as it is called, was cut by a college boy who was punished by being kept from going home at the end of term. An elaboration of the story says that the same boy composed the school song, *Domum*, which is sung at the end of each term. Chained to a tree, he was found dead when the school returned.

It has also been suggested that the song was composed by boys in the year of the Winchester plague, 1666, when the college was sent for safety to a farm a few miles from the city.

The twice-daily ritual of 'Hills' was abolished in 1868 but the tradition lingers on, as college boys still mount the hill at the beginning of the winter and summer terms. In fact, these are the only occasions in the school year when the college meets regularly as a body, at 8 o'clock in the morning on the top of St Catherine's Hill!

In 1930 the college bought the hill from the Ecclesiastical Commissioners and today it is managed as a nature reserve by the Hampshire and Isle of Wight Naturalists Trust, who keep it clear of the scrub that would otherwise smother its rich flora of chalkland flowers and herbs.

Alfred's Great Works

'Winchester returned to urban life in the reign of Alfred, as the largest of the fortified places designed to defend Wessex from Danish attack.'

— Martin Biddle and Derek Keene

The grid of streets in the centre of Winchester is basically the same as that laid out more than a thousand years ago by Alfred, King of the West Saxons.

The High Street and the Broadway make up the spine of the city, and are served by St Georges Street and Clements Street as 'back access'. At right-angles run cross-links such as Parchment Street, St Thomas Street and the three Brook Streets — Upper, Middle and Lower.

One street of the old Saxon city is 'fossilised' under the site of the Norman castle to the south of the West Gate. Excavations have revealed substantial standing remains of some of the fifty houses that were hastily buried by the new conquerors.

The Saxon city fostered by Alfred was the largest of thirty-three *burhs* which he set up in Wessex, throughout much of present-day Southern England — beyond Exeter in the west, Hastings in the east and Oxford in the north.

Each *burh* was well defended, and in the case of Winchester and some other places it was planned so that within the walls a variety of trades and crafts could be pursued in safety, thereby preserving what we would call 'civilised life'.

For Winchester it was a second great phase of civic activity, the first being the Roman walled town *Venta Belgarum*, established in the 1st Century AD. This earlier foundation still underlies much of the city, but enough has been excavated to know that the Forum lay to the north of the cathedral, between the City Museum and the Wessex Hotel.

The Saxons almost certainly made use of the existing Roman defences, as indicated by a remarkable document called the Burghal Hidage which gives details of Alfred's *burhs*. This shows that the length of the city's perimeter (about two miles) was almost exactly the same as that of the Roman settlement.

Although Winchester was clearly an important town in Roman times, remarkably little is known of this period. It was connected by five roads to other important centres, including Old Sarum (still called Sarum Road), Silchester and the port Clausentum, now in the Bitterne district of Southampton. It was the fifth largest town in Roman Britain, a military station, an administrative and commercial centre for the Belgae, and it probably also had a substantial weaving works.

Roman Winchester probably reached its peak in the late 3rd and early 4th centuries AD, when it contained elaborate town houses and all the other requirements of civilised living. The town spread beyond the walls to nearby places such as Winnall and the northern suburbs and Highcliffe in the southeast. Further afield, there were settlements at Owslebury and a villa at Sparsholt. A virtually complete mosaic has been excavated from the latter in recent years and can be seen in the City Museum.

After the collapse of the Roman Empire in the late 4th century, the town decayed and many of the stone buildings that had once stood became replaced by timber-framed wattle-and-daub structures. A fascinating insight into the last years of Roman rule has come from recent excavations of several hundred graves in a Roman cemetery at Lankhills to the north of the city. Several of these have been shown to be the earliest known 'Saxon' graves in Britain, and as such may represent the remains of Germanic mercenaries who came to Winchester and the 'frontier region' of the Upper Thames to help maintain civic order.

Even though Winchester undoubtedly decayed into an 'urban village' as Roman rule gave way to the Saxon incursions of the so-called Dark Ages, it must have retained some of its urban importance, for in the year 662 AD Cenwalh, King of Wessex, transferred his bishopric from

Dorchester-on-Thames to Winchester, where a royal church had been built some 14 years before.

With hindsight this event can be seen as the step which established the future of Winchester as a major royal and ecclesiastical centre. Within a generation of the first conversion of the West Saxon King, Cynegils, father of Cenwalh, Winchester had become a focus for the faith that was to mould the birth of England. It became the capital of the West Saxon kings, whose remains are said still to be in the mortuary chests in the cathedral.

The period between Cenwalh and Alfred was a time when small Saxon kingdoms became subject to overlordships and there eventually emerged a single figure who can be called the first English King. It is a complicated subject beyond the scope of this book, but nonetheless important because it was at Winchester that English power eventually settled, making it the first capital of England. Alfred's great-grandson Edgar (959-75) is regarded as the first King of All England, though Alfred himself undoubtedly acted as leader of the English forces which stemmed Viking attacks in the latter part of the 9th century.

Despite its proximity to the South Coast, Winchester seems only to have suffered one major Viking raid, in 860, when Alfred was only a boy. A large army of pagans laid waste the city and made off with 'immense booty'. However, before they could reach their ships they were intercepted by a combined force of men from Hampshire and Berkshire, who were 'masters of the battlefield' and cut down as many men as they could.

Winchester also saw the quieter phase of Alfred's life that came after he had secured his kingdom in 878, when he 'put aside the sword' and sought to improve the fortunes of his people by encouraging learning and better public administration.

The statue of Alfred which dominates the east side of the city unfortunately only depicts the warring side of his character. Perched high on a great plinth of granite, it was erected in 1901, when the city staged an elaborate Millenary Celebration of the 'popular date' of his death. Scholars now believe that he in fact died in 899, but no matter, Winchester paid her respects and raised a tangible tribute to a great citizen.

The palace where Alfred lived probably lies a short distance to the west of the cathedral. Here he planned a kingdom that could defend itself and pursued a life of letters: he was, in essence, the first publisher, editor and author to work in the English language.

Aware that most of his subjects could not read the Latin in which all books were then written he decided to translate and rewrite some of the classics in everyday Anglo-Saxon. Some of these monkish

The King Alfred statue by Sir Hamo Thornycroft, erected in The Broadway in 1901

manuscripts still exist, including a translation of a manual for the guidance of parish priests, Gregory's *Pastoral Care.*

In the preface of this work Alfred explains how he sought the help of churchmen to understand the original Latin: 'When I had learnt it so that I understood it, and so that I could quite clearly give its meaning, I turned it into English.' He then produced copies of the translation and sent one to each bishopric.

One of his closest aides was the Welsh monk Asser, who spent six months of the year in his household and subsequently wrote a *Life of King Alfred*, the first biography of a lay Englishman.

Alfred also produced an edition of Bede's *Ecclesiastical History of the English* and another great work on the history and geography of the world, based on an earlier work by a Spanish cleric. He added a good deal of new material, including the tales of Scandinavian travellers who came to the royal court and gave Alfred first-hand reports to add to his 'copy'. No doubt he also made use of his own considerable knowledge of Europe, which he had first visited as a boy of four.

Amongst the other great works which he inspired was the Doom Book (not to be confused with the Domesday Book), a manual of English law which was kept at Winchester. He is also credited with the *Anglo-Saxon Chronicle*, which gathered together the story of the Saxon colonisation of Britain and continued to record major events for another three hundred years.

Alfred was very generous to the church, not only within his own kingdom, but also in such places as Brittany and Ireland. In old age he furthered the church in Winchester, where the Old Minster had stood for more than two hundred years. With his Queen he founded the Nun's Minster (or Nunnaminster), which stood to the south of the Alfred statue and is recalled by the names Abbey Gardens and Abbey Mill.

He also laid plans for the New Minster, which was built after his death by his son, Edward the Elder. It stood extremely close to the northern wall of the Old Minster (obviously before the advent of Town Planning!) and eventually became the resting place of Alfred's remains.

After the Conquest the monks of the New Minster moved to a new building outside the city, at Hyde, where the gatehouse still stands. In 1110, in solemn procession, they took with them the bones of Alfred; but the burial site of this great man was irretrievably lost during the demolition of the abbey at the Reformation.

The only relic that remains today is the simple stone which probably marked his grave at Hyde Abbey and was spotted in a garden in St Peter Street in the late 18th century. It can now be seen in the City Museum. The lead coffins of Alfred and his son are said to have been discovered at about the same time by workmen, who sold them for a few guineas.

Riddles of the Old Minster

'The Benedictine monks of Winchester created, under the patronage of Aethelwold, manuscripts of the finest quality.'
— Saxon Festival Souvenir Brochure, 1984

One of the most astonishing discoveries made in recent years in Winchester has been the site of the Old Minster, which the Normans demolished and replaced with the existing cathedral.

The final form of this Saxon church was due to a remarkable bishop, Aethelwold, who was born in Winchester and became one of the most important figures in the great flowering of English art and literature that occurred during the 10th century.

Aethelwold served at Glastonbury and was the abbot of Abingdon but eventually came back to his home town in 963 to be consecrated by Dunstan, Archbishop of Canterbury. He was strongly influenced by Benedictine monastic reform on the Continent, which insisted on strict adherence to the Rule. Yet at the Old Minster he found a state of wild dissipation, with the monks enjoying all the pleasures of the flesh, so he decided to replace them with brethren from Abingdon: according to one version of the story, the new men lined up in the close to take the places of their 'fallen' brothers!

Aethelwold's life was recorded by the contemporary poet Wulfstan, whose work has long been thought to contain obscure passages describing the Old Minster, such as:

> He also added many chapels with sacred altars which keep the entry of threshhold doubtful, so that whoever walks. . . cannot tell whence he comes or whither to return, since open doors are seen on every hand, nor does any certain path of a way appear.

Many of the 'riddles' of passages such as these have been clarified in recent years by the excavations of Professor Martin Biddle and his colleagues, which have shown that the Old Minster was, literally, fantastic.

They found that in the final quarter of the 10th century the existing

The Old Minster: an impression drawn by the late David White of the County Architect's Department and based on information provided by the Winchester Research Unit (Courtesy of the Winchester Excavations Committee)

The foundations of the Old Minster outlined on the turf at the northwest corner of the cathedral. St Swithun's grave is marked by the square stone at the west end
(Courtesy of Murray Davison)

Old Minster was more than doubled in length (i.e. to about half the length of the present cathedral) and was elaborated in a most curious way.

The original 7th century cross-shaped building was first extended at the west end to join up with an isolated tower. The structure was also given large 'ear-pieces' or transepts and enclosed the grave of its patron saint, St Swithun, a celebrated Winchester bishop whose shrine drew crowds of pilgrims to the city (see p. 32).

Then the small east end was extended with a crypt and semi-circular side chambers. It is hardly surprising that the innocent worshipper was unable to decide 'whence he comes or whither he returns'!

The Old Minster was extraordinary in other ways, too, if Wulfstan can be believed. He says that it had an organ with 400 pipes which was played with two separate keyboards and had blowers operated by 70 men. They stamped on bellows and shouted and cheered to spur each other on to greater efforts.

The organ has gone and the Old Minster is today a shadow on the turf beside the cathedral. However, there are some relics of Aethelwold and the energy that made Winchester at this time one of the prime centres of European culture.

The most outstanding of these is the *Benedictional*, a fabulously decorated religious manuscript prepared during the late 10th century by the monks of St Swithun's in the cells of their writing room or *scriptorium*.
It is in the British Library in London where its lush pages show the acanthus fronds and gold leaf that were characteristic of the style of the Winchester School of Illumination.

A poem in Latin at the beginning of the book says that Aethelwold commanded that the book was to have 'many frames well adorned and filled with various figures decorated with numerous beautiful colours and with gold.' The framework was characteristic of the Winchester School, which also involved pastel shades contrasted with rich golds, purples, greens and blues.

The text was written in gold in a lovely rounded hand called Carolingian Miniscule after its roots in the Byzantine world. The revival of calligraphy in the early part of this century by Edward Johnston, who developed a style called Foundational Hand, owed its inspiration to the craft of the monks of the *scriptorium* at Winchester and elsewhere.

The survival of the *Benedictional* is itself a miracle, for it might easily have been destroyed during the Civil War, yet it survived and was rediscovered in 1720, in the hands of the Duke of Devonshire.

The influence of the Winchester School also extended to metalwork, carving, jewellery and embroidery. Durham Cathedral owns a rare example of an elaborately decorated priest's stole or maniple which was made in Winchester in the early years of the 10th century. Discovered in the tomb of St Cuthbert, it shows figures of the prophets separated by acanthus fronds.

Ten years ago the contents of a cess-pit in the west of the city revealed a rare 11th century 'reliquary', a flask-shaped, gilt-bronze container for carrying relics during religious processions. Examination with X-rays has shown fragments of parchment and traces of the relics themselves — perhaps hair, bone or dust made sacred by contact with a saint's shrine. It is now on display in the City Museum.

The Conqueror Comes to Town

'Although William appreciated the growing importance of London, he nevertheless regarded Winchester as the real capital of England.'

— W. Lloyd Woodland

In the month following the Battle of Hastings the Norman conquerors under William, Duke of Normandy, came to Winchester to secure their kingdom. The city was in the hands of Edward the Confessor's widow Edith, who decided to surrender and sent out local citizens with gifts to meet the victors.

William and his army then marched on to London and two months later, on Christmas Day, he was crowned at Westminster. It was not until Whitsun 1068 that he was crowned in Aethelwold's Old Minster at Winchester. Thereafter he 'wore the crown' in the Wessex capital at Easter each year.

Local citizens have often been depicted as 'shivering in their shoes' at the thought of what the new king might exact, particularly since the bodies of the abbot of the New Minster, an uncle of King Harold, and some of his monks had been discovered on the battlefield, wearing chainmail over their clerical habits.

The victor is often quoted as saying: 'The abbot is worth a barony, and every monk a manor' — in French, of course, since he never managed to master the native tongue. The New Minster was, in fact, inconvenienced by the construction of the Conqueror's palace nearby but the Domesday Book reveals that the monastery remained extremely

The north transept of the cathedral, showing the Romanesque style of the original Norman building
(Courtesy of John Crook)

well endowed, with twenty-two lordships of manors.

Compiled in 1086 in Winchester, but excluding the city itself, the Domesday survey also showed that a mere five per cent of the total landed wealth of England was held by Englishmen. In Hampshire alone the Norman Hugh de Port, whose principal seat was at Basing, held 55

The Domesday Book being 'written up' in Winchester in 1086: a display created by the Ivor Heal Design Company for the Domesday 900 Exhibition.

lordships, while the King himself held 67.

The exact movements of William after his victory are not known, but an ingenious study of the Domesday values of manors in North Hampshire and elsewhere is said to show that the needs of the new king and his army were so great that the effects were still apparent many years later.

On this basis, it has been suggested that it was at Easton a few miles to the east of the Winchester that he joined reinforcements landed on the South Coast and obtained the surrender of the city before turning to London and the north.

Certainly there seems to have been no opposition locally, and indeed churchmen were no doubt keen to acquiesce to the change in secular power, whilst laymen might have hoped for a shift of power in their favour. William believed that he had a better claim to the throne than Harold who was elected by the Witan after the death of Edward the Confessor. As one historian has put it: 'On the whole it seems that William's monarchy was Edward's run at full power.'

In Winchester that power was quickly expressed in several ways. On the western heights of the city the Normans built a castle, 'bulldozing' its foundations on top of the very streets and houses that Alfred had established in the city nearly two hundred years before.

Hampshire people are forever reminded of this ancient site of power, for it is still called The Castle and now includes the offices of the County Council and the Law Courts, though little remains of the Norman works.

Here the Conqueror imprisoned Stigand, the last Saxon Bishop of Winchester, a man who was also Archbishop of Canterbury and was tainted by holding several other church offices at the same time.

A most important function of the castle was as a 'bank', a place where the royal treasure could be safely stored. Indeed, at this time Winchester had more moneyers — the men who struck the coinage — than London.

William's palace covered a large area roughly from outside the west end of the cathedral to the High Street. He doubled the extent of the former Saxon palace by building on a hall and other buildings to the north. Much of the new land was seized from the New Minster and a dozen Saxon householders with scant if any compensation.

Old house deeds referring to 'the constabulary' still echo the royal ownership of this part of the city, between Great Minster Street and Little Minster Street: their occupants paid rents to that important royal official, the Constable of the Castle.

A more substantial reminder of Norman Winchester is the curfew bell which is still rung at eight o'clock each evening from the tower of the 'Old Guildhall', now Lloyds Bank. An earlier bell was ordered to be sounded by the Conqueror, presumably to keep townsfolk in their place by encouraging them to cover their fires and retire to bed (Fr: *couvre-feu*).

The greatest Norman building in the city is, of course, the cathedral, but this was not started until thirteen years after the Conquest. It was masterminded by Bishop Walkelin, a relative of William's, who lived to see its dedication in 1093. Its opening was attended by almost all the dignitaries of the English church, who filed in solemn procession from the New Minster into the Old and then into the new cathedral, bearing the shrine of St Swithun (see p. 33).

The original architecture of the cathedral is best seen in the north and south transepts, where the raw curved arches of the Norman builders are unaltered. It was, it must be said, somewhat jerry-built and experts say that the workmanship is not the best. Within fourteen years the central tower had fallen down.

However, by any standards the cathedral was an amazing achievement and should be compared with the more protracted creations of today, such as Liverpool Cathedral. Walkelin was clearly a hustler: his determination is evident in a much-told story of Hampage Wood, which still stands between Winchester and Alresford. In reply to a request for timber for the new church, the king told the bishop to take as much as he could in three days. Walkelin interpreted the permission literally and is said to have cleared the entire wood with an army of axeman.

The cathedral was, at one time, even longer than it appears to be, for it extended about 40 feet further west.

When it was built it was with one exception the longest church in Christendom and is today the longest medieval cathedral in the world. Its later Gothic nave (see p. 41) is also unsurpassed.

William Rufus and his Machiavellian Aide

'When you stand and look down on the tomb of William Rufus you cannot help but wonder how so hated a man came to be given so beautiful a memorial.'

— Brian Vesey-Fitzgerald

In August 1868 in Winchester Cathedral the plain but moving tomb thought to be that of William Rufus, son of the Conqueror, was opened and amongst the contents was found an iron tip which could have been that which pierced the king's breast in that well-known hunting incident in the New Forest.

There were also pieces of gold braid, the carved head of the wand of the kind traditionally buried with the king and the bones of a short thickset man who died in middle age.

These findings seemed to establish that the Purbeck marble tomb, which now rests at the foot of the choir steps, was that of the Norman king who, says a chronicler, was buried 'with a concourse of many chiefs but with the grief of few'.

However, there must be some doubt because the remains of William Rufus are also said to be in one of the famous mortuary chests that rest on the presbytery screens in the cathedral. Although antiquarians have been tempted to ascribe the tomb in the choir to William Rufus, they have had difficulty in explaining how he can, so to speak, be buried in two places at once!

When Rufus and his companions rode out to the New Forest from Winchester on that day in the year 1100, probably from the castle, they were embarking on a popular pursuit of both Saxon and Norman kings. It combined fun and adventure and helped to stock up the larder.

The question of whether he was killed accidently or on purpose will probably never be solved. Even the site, marked with a 'stone' in the New Forest, is in doubt and some favour a theory that he was in fact skewered near Beaulieu.

One theory, advanced in recent years, is that William Rufus was killed by his brother Henry so that he could marry the royal Saxon, Edith, who eventually did become his queen. She was a nun at Romsey Abbey and, so the theory goes, was kept there at the behest of William Rufus.

But the simplest explanation of all, that it was an unfortunate hunting accident is perhaps the easiest to believe, for two of his kinsmen had been killed in a similar manner.

Yet the idea that William Rufus was murdered is attractive because he has such a reputation for being a foul king. It was even claimed by the populace that the burial of such a godless man as Rufus in the cathedral was responsible for the collapse of the central tower seven years later.

One of Rufus's principal aides was Randolf Flambard, an obscure priest-cum-lawyer who rose to be the king's chief adviser and Abbot of the New Minster, and later Bishop of Durham. For more than a decade he had been the evil genius behind Machiavellian schemes to enrich the royal treasury — and his own pockets — by withholding church appointments.

He lived in a splendid house outside the North Gate of the city which, with typical arrogance, he built over a street — probably a continuation of Swan Lane. Yet the clever-ruthless side of his character which is usually depicted is hard to reconcile with the beauty of the churches he built at Christchurch and Durham.

It is also difficult to obtain a true picture of William Rufus. He is in one instance depicted in the *Anglo-Saxon Chronicle* doling out the contents of the royal treasury to monasteries, as instructed by his father, and in another demanding back a grant of money made during sickness to Bishop Walkelin because he had recovered!

The aged prelate himself died ten days later without abiding by the request and it has been suggested that he hid the treasure. In 1833 a cache of nine thousand new-minted silver pennies of William I were discovered by boys playing in a field a few miles outside Winchester, at Beauworth, whose manor was held by the bishop. Were they perhaps the missing treasure or were they buried during an invasion scare?

After the death of Rufus the English throne was claimed by his brother Henry, who rode to Winchester with the main purpose of seizing the royal treasure. He then continued to London, where he was crowned. The history books have been kinder to him, largely because he renewed the status quo by restoring to the churches the control of their finances.

As a mark of these kinder times, Anselm, Archbishop of Canterbury, who had quarrelled bitterly with William Rufus in Winchester, was recalled from exile. For his part, Flambard fled to Normandy and tried to oust Henry by supporting the claim to the throne of his brother Robert.

For some townsfolk of Winchester the accession of Henry was perhaps not such a boon. In 1110 he instructed the bishop to compile a survey of Winchester, part of the so-called Winton Domesday. This made it possible for the king to check that all fees due to him were being paid.

The Winton Domesday shows that most people still lived within the walls of the city, though there were considerable suburbs, particularly beyond the West Gate. The old names of many of Winchester's streets are also revealed. The little street below the Law Courts, now Trafalgar Street, was called Gar Street, Southgate Street was Gold Street, whilst St Thomas Street was Calpe Street.

The citizens of Winchester, in common with those of London, almost certainly started to obtain certain freedoms at this time, although the original city charter is now lost.

The city was run according to custom endorsed by the meeting three times a year of the burghmote, a body of the principal citizens. The main officer of local government was the king's reeve, who collected local taxes, including such measures as a penny a week from each butcher's shop. He rendered an account to the sheriff of Hampshire, who in turn accounted for the city's farm, its contribution to the exchequer.

Later, in the 13th century, individual streets or pairs of streets were under the control of aldermen, who administered their own courts. Householders had the responsibility of looking out for breaches of the peace, while beadles acted as the forerunners of policemen.

The ruins of the medieval palace of Wolvesey, seen from St Giles's Hill, showing (from left to right) Wymond's Tower and 'the keep' of the East Hall, with the gable of the chapel beyond

Wolvesey Palace and Family Infighting

'If at any one period it became clear that Winchester was no longer a royal capital it was during the reign of Stephen.'

— Martin Biddle and Derek Keene

Although Winchester has generally managed to avoid the worst of wars, there was a time in the middle of the 12th century when its bishop became involved in a bitter tussle for the crown which resulted in vast areas of the city being devastated.

The bishop was Henry of Blois, grandson of William the Conqueror and an important figure in the struggle between Stephen, his brother, and Matilda, the rightful heir to the throne of Henry I.

During a fiery battle in 1141 much of the centre of Winchester was destroyed, including the Conqueror's Palace and no less than forty churches and two abbeys, according to some chroniclers' reports.

The ruins of Wolvesey in the south-east quarter of Winchester are all that remain of the great palace-cum-castle that Bishop Henry fortified to match his importance and the strife of the times, though its ruination was a much later event. In the Siege of Winchester, as these troubled events have been called, Bishop Henry and mercenaries hired for the purpose took up positions at Wolvesey and in the Conqueror's Palace. On higher land to the west in the castle was the Empress Matilda with her troops and followers.

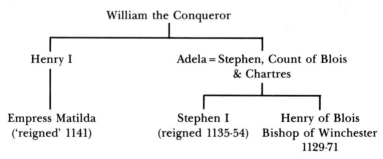

In the ensuing battle Matilda was routed and forced to flee west in disarray, pursued by forces of her namesake, Stephen's queen. Making over open country for Wherwell in the Test Valley, the empress's knights shed armour and abandoned valuables in their haste to escape.

Both parties in the siege had cause to be bitter. Earlier in the year, only six years after Winchester had welcomed Stephen as their king,

Wolvesey Palace, the surviving wing of the bishop's house started in the 17th century, with the attached chapel of the medieval palace in the background

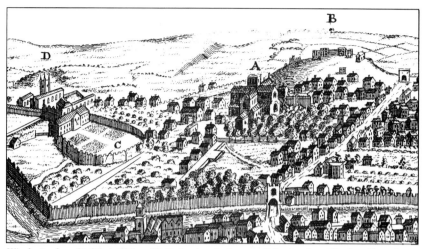

Winchester from St Giles's Hill, a detail showing the baroque bishop's palace (C), the college (D), the King's House (B) and many other features noted in 1723 by the antiquarian William Stukeley (Courtesy of The Printed Page, Winchester)

Matilda had entered the city in a joyful procession of 'the great and the good' to be blessed in the cathedral by Bishop Henry and others. More importantly, she had taken possession of the treasure and the crown in the castle.

Later events in London, however, had gone against her accession and she had been forced to flee the capital — at which point Bishop Henry had decided that the noble lady, whose haughtiness rankled, was a liability and he retreated for safety to Winchester.

He was bitter because he had helped to gain the coronation of his brother, yet had failed to secure the rewards he had expected. Although he became the pope's legate, the supreme churchman in England, he would dearly have loved the Archbishopric of Canterbury. Stephen, who feared his power, had prudently declined to secure him this position.

Later, when a change of Pope lost him his legateship, Henry of Blois tried — and almost succeeded — in having Winchester made an archbishopric. There was a good deal of sense in this, for the diocese was huge and then stretched from South London to the South Coast. But his manoeuvrings, which would have involved elevating the Abbot of Hyde to a bishopric, did not quite come off due to yet another papal death.

During the family infighting of Stephen and Matilda the changes of loyalty made by Bishop Henry must have been marvellous to witness: he was in fact 'three-faced' in the business. Only months before his men were preparing to lob firebrands at Matilda and her men in the castle he had called a church council at Winchester to explain to fellow bishops why he had then deserted Stephen's cause.

Saying that he had the peace of the country at heart and that he had thought that the rightful heir would never claim her rights, he then painted a lurid picture of Stephen's 'misdeeds' and declared: 'While I should love my mortal brother, I should esteem far more highly the cause of my immortal Father.'

Now he had once more switched his loyalties, back to Stephen, and would soon have to argue once more that, after all, his brother had his support. It is hardly surprising that when Stephen died and was succeeded by Matilda's son, Henry II, Bishop Henry had to flee the country!

In his absence his half-dozen castles, including that at Merdon, near Hursley, were 'destroyed', like the other thousand or so 'unofficial' fortifications that had sprung up during the anarchy of the times. Although a similar fate was ordered for Wolvesey it escaped, presumably as it was the traditional seat of the bishop.

Bishop Henry fled to Cluny in France, where he had once served as a monk, sending his treasure in advance. His exile was, however, short and he soon returned to Hampshire where he spent the rest of his life administering his diocese. He is noted for his support of the arts and amongst the relics of his time is the magnificent Winchester Bible, kept in the Cathedral Library, and a beautiful Psalter decorated with miniatures which is in the British Museum.

During his term of office the huge black Tournai marble font beside the north aisle of the cathedral was also set up in Winchester; its stone came from quarries in Belgium. One of the traditional stories depicted in the relief carving on the font, which is dedicated to St Nicholas, tells the gruesome tale of the innkeeper in the midst of a famine who made sausage meat from the bodies of three young boys. Fortunately, the good saint turned up for a night's stay and restored the children to life.

In the cathedral Bishop Henry is also remembered as the prelate who gathered up from the crypt the remains of the Saxon kings and bishops which had been brought there from the Old Minster. As already mentioned, in the 16th century they were placed in chests on the top of the choir screens. Those above the south presbytery aisle are reputed to include the bones of Rufus, as well as the kings Cynegils, Ethelwulf and Edred, while to the north are the remains of such men as Kenulph and Egbert, 'the first King of England' (a dubious claim), and grandfather of Alfred the Great.

The most enduring of the bishop's Winchester works is the Hospital of St Cross (see p. 76).

Strangely, for a man of such power and wealth as Bishop Henry, there is no trace of his tomb in the cathedral, though remains found in front of the high altar, including a crozier and a bishop's ring, may mark the site of his grave.

A Medieval Moneyspinner —
St Giles's Fair

'Some of the most profitable investments were the shops on St Giles's Hill...'
— Barbara Carpenter Turner

Anyone who has been to a large trade show would instantly recognise the excitement of the great fair that took over Winchester and the surrounding area each September during the Middle Ages.

It was staged on St Giles's Hill, the prominent escarpment which rises at the east end of the High Street, where merchants from many parts of England and the Continent gathered to trade their wares. So many traders came down from London that the legal business of the capital was suspended during 'the fair at Winchester'.

The brow of the hill is now an extremely pleasant public park with a superb view of all the main sights of the city. The higher slopes were built over during the last century to create a suburb, which has become much sought after.

Cloth, wool and livestock were the mainstays of St Giles's Fair, but there was also trade in leather, furs, spices from the Orient, secondhand clothes(!) and a wide variety of 'impulse buys', including pet animals such as monkeys, bears and peacocks.

Many of the merchants brought their ships to the thriving medieval port of Southampton, while others travelled large distances with packhorse, often at risk from robbers. A notorious danger spot on the London road was the heavily wooded 'Pass of Alton', now an innocuous part of the A31 between Froyle and Bentley. The Statute of Westminster framed by Edward I improved the lot of merchants travelling to the fair, by allowing a 'bowshot' of clear land on either side of the highway.

Winchester's great annual event was an important source of church income and probably originated from a purely local fair. It was assigned to the bishop by that profane monarch William Rufus, who at the end of the 11th century granted him the right to hold a fair lasting three days. It proved so profitable that it was progressively extended to sixteen days. The huge site on the hill was laid out with semi-permanent shops, arranged in streets according to the trades and nationalities of the merchants.

A surprisingly barren St Giles's Hill, photographed in the 1920s
(Courtesy of the Hampshire County Library)

These included Fullers' Street, Grey Cloths' Street, Parmenters' Row, Exeter Street, Skinners' Row, Wool Street, French Street and many more. The exact layout of the fair is not known, though it centred around the chapel of St Giles and its cemetery.

The church made its money from tolls levied during the 'period of entry' and fines and ensured a trade monopoly by taking over the city and an area of 'seven leagues' around (about ten miles). This at first included the whole of the town of Southampton. Strict rules of trade were enforced, including checks on the quality of wine and beer.

The fair was administered from the Bishop's Pavilion Court, which became corrupted over the years to Palm Hall, a name which is borne by a new street and one of the houses on the hill. The start and finish of the fair was accompanied by lengthy ceremonies which emphasised the takeover of civic powers by the bishop and his officers from the mayor and bailiffs of the city. All civil cases within the ten-mile orbit of the fair were, for example, taken out of the hands of municipal authorities or lords of the manor and tried by a church court.

The handover started at sunrise on the 31st August, the eve of St Giles's Day, when the Judge of the Bishop's Pavilion Court and the Treasurer rode out from the bishop's palace at Wolvesey to the King's Gate, which still stands, where the mayor and his officers were waiting to deliver the keys of the city. A proclamation made clear that 'the bishop was boss'.

It read:

> Let no merchant or other for these sixteen days within a circuit of
> seven leagues round the fair, sell, buy or set out for sale any
> merchandise in any place other than the fair under penalty of
> forfeiture of goods to the Bishop.

The city also surrendered the 'tron', a great weighing machine for wool,
which was taken up to the hill for the duration of the fair. The return
of the tron was a good excuse for merrymaking and the city accounts
contain several references to money spent on this essential ceremonial.

The fair required a regulated system of weights and measures and
perhaps for this reason examples of some of the earliest standards survive
in the city. These include a fine set of weights issued for use with wool
and other bulky goods after the statute of 1340 defined the avoirdupois
system, which led later to the modern (but now obsolescent!) English
pound weight. The largest of the Winchester measures weighs ninety-
one pounds, the equivalent of a quarter of a sack of wool.

Standards were revised in the reign of Henry VII towards the end
of the 15th century. The city owns a number of measures from this time,
including the 'Winchester Bushel' (800 Troy ounces of wheat), which
was not replaced until the introduction of the British Imperial Gallon
in 1824. The city also owns the oldest surviving standard yard, an example
of which was sent by Henry VII to all major towns and cities. It is a
mere four-hundredths of an inch shorter than its modern equivalent!

After the fair had finished many merchants 'descended' to the city
to continue trading and on some occasions there was so much unfinished
business that the fair was allowed to run on.

The proceedings were not, however, all business. There were no doubt
jugglers, dancers, acrobats, fire-eaters, sword-swallowers, strong men,
bearded women and two-headed monstrosities. And to provide
something to watch while the ale slid down there were mystery plays,
traditional performances that blended the Biblical and the bawdy.

Such a hot-house atmosphere needed a strong hand to control it and
the bishop and his bailiffs had to work for their money. But the rewards
were substantial and the Chapter House and much of the Cathedral
Close were built and maintained on the profits.

The austere lives of Winchester's monks were also enlivened by this
annual event. A 14th century document describing the duties of the
officers of St Swithun's Priory gives the cellarer the important task of
keepering the 'animals acquired from time to time by the brethren', who
no doubt obtained them at the fair.

The heyday of St Giles's Fair was during the 13th century, though it
fell off sharply in the final years. The reasons are obscure, but were

probably related to changing patterns of the wool trade. Nonetheless, it continued to be held, increasingly on a local basis only, until at least the early years of the last century.

The present 'pleasure ground' on the hill was bought from the Ecclesiastical Commissioners in 1878, while the upper lands were generously donated sixteen years later by Lord Northbrook, a member of the Baring family. The mayor at the time was a well-known Winchester architect, Thomas Stopher, who had designed many of the imposing houses which already stood on the hill.

Swithun, the Saint who Drew the Crowds

'As noisy a crowd of pilgrims
As ever wore out shoe leather on a short cut to Heaven.'

— Patrick B. Mace

There is a strong tradition that during the Middle Ages Winchester was visited by large numbers of pilgrims seeking the shrine of St Swithun.

They flocked to the city from London and other parts of the country and even from overseas, perhaps visiting other shrines along the way. The Old Minster made the best of the cult, extending its dedication to the saint who once had been its prior and was bishop of the diocese during 852-62. The New Minster founded by King Alfred also had its shrine, dedicated to St Josse, though it was always a very poor second to St Swithun's.

One of the best-known pilgrims was Henry II, who ensured that the cult of Swithun would become even more celebrated when he landed at Southampton and travelled on to Winchester to confess his murder of Thomas à Becket. He then continued to Canterbury 'like a common pilgrim'.

The Pilgrims Way between the two cathedral cities has become particularly well known in modern times through the efforts of writers such as Hilaire Belloc. In his *The Old Road* he describes his speculative attempts to trace the route. In fact, many people now believe that the Pilgrims Way is largely a romantic invention of the Victorian age, though no doubt some pilgrims did follow in the footsteps of Henry II.

St Swithun's shrine itself was, however, very definitely not an invention:

countless pilgrims trod the road to Winchester and helped to maintain a steady income for the priory and cathedral. They came at first to the Old Minster and later to the north transept of the cathedral, entering a door which can still be seen in the south-west corner. Here they paid their dues, purchased a taper or relic and then made their way behind the choir to the shrine.

Originally the relics were kept in the 'Holy Hole' or feretory, a small chamber behind the alter, where pilgrims would stretch out their hands to touch them. At the beginning of the 13th century the popularity of St Swithun had grown to such an extent that the east end of the cathedral was extended and a Lady Chapel added.

The shuffling line of pilgrims slowly made its way to the shrine, which bore hundreds of lighted candles. On the walls of this part of the cathedral were hung the crutches of those who had found a cure. It is an atmosphere that can easily be imagined by anyone who has visited Lourdes or one of the other centres of pilgrimage that still exist on the Continent.

The pilgrims could only visit a very limited part of the cathedral, which was principally the church where the monks of the priory carried out their devotions. An iron gate which barred entrance to the south transept from the east end still stands close to its original position; it is reputed to be the oldest surviving example of medieval decorated wrought ironwork in the country.

The reputation of St Swithun, who was a native of Winchester, helped to make the city a place that people sought long after it had ceased to have any great importance in the affairs of the country. Even the efforts of Henry VIII's officers in 1538 to erase memories of the saint by destroying the relics and melting down the metalwork did not succeed totally.

In 1962 to mark the 1100th anniversary of the saint's death the site of the shrine in the cathedral was marked with a new canopy and grille. This was dedicated in the presence of the Bishop and Dean of Stavanger Cathedral, Norway, which was dedicated to Swithun by a Winchester monk in the 12th century.

During subsequent excavations of the Cathedral Yard to the north of the cathedral the original site of the saint's grave was found and is now marked by a plain slab.

Ironically, the reputation of St Swithun for humility and kindness brought him the sort of popular fame that he would no doubt have disliked. It also meant that his remains were shunted from place to place as the topography of the cathedral precinct changed.

At his request he was first buried in the churchyard of the original Old Minster. Very soon there were reports of the ground splitting open

The east end of the cathedral, built in the 13th century to replace the original Norman apse and also to provide more room inside for pilgrims visiting the shrine of St Swithun

and people started to seek miracles by lying on the spot. After the rebuilding of the Old Minster in the late 10th century the grave was opened and the saint's remains taken inside the church.

The well-known traditional rhyme concerning the weather to be expected after the 15th of July is related to a lengthy spell of wet weather that is supposed to have upset these plans:

St Swithun's Day, if thou be fair,
For forty days it will remain.
St Swithun's Day, if thou bring rain,
For forty days it will remain.

The final journey for the saint's bones was in solemn procession to the Norman cathedral to dedicate the new building in 1093. Demolition of the Old Minster, which revealed more relics of St. Swithun, was started the very next day, according to the chroniclers. This enabled the Norman masons to finish their task, for the old and the new churches overlapped at the west end.

Surprisingly, the nave of the cathedral is not due east-west but dips substantially to the south. This unusual orientation was necessary to fit its vast bulk between the royal palace to the west and the New Minster precinct to the north.

St Swithun's reputation rested upon his character as a 'good man', but more than that he was by all accounts a superb teacher; much of Alfred's liking for letters is traditionally attributed to the saint's influence at the court of his father, the West Saxon King, Aethelwulf.

Miraculous happenings were attributed to St Swithun, including an occasion when he is said to have made broken eggs whole — which is why the new canopy is decorated with eggshells. In another instance, during the building of Aethelwold's minster, a workman fell to the ground and was taken for dead but made a wonderful recovery.

At a more mundane level, the citizens of Winchester have cause to thank him for the first bridge, a forerunner of the present City Bridge, which ran from the old walled city to the Soke, an area in which the bishop's jurisdiction was paramount until 1835.

The one reminder of the days when Catholic travellers sought spiritual comfort in Winchester is the name of Pilgrims School, the prep school for choirboys (both for the cathedral and Winchester College) which stands in the Cathedral Close. Although Winchester had earlier cathedral schools, Pilgrims is a modern foundation dating only from 1931 and was given its name to mark the tradition that religious travellers sought food and shelter in the Pilgrims Hall, a fine 13th century structure used by the school. However, it has also been suggested that the hall was used by the cathedral priory for commercial or agricultural purposes.

The Great Hall and Early Parliaments

'Parliament was not devised on the sudden to perpetuate a revolution. . . It grew up gradually. .'
— G.M. Trevelyan

One of Winchester's most intriguing sights, painted on the east wall of the medieval castle's Great Hall in the last century, is the year-by-year listing of Hampshire's parliamentary representatives.

This is appropriate for a building which was involved in the earliest stirrings of the English parliamentary system. Several assemblies were held here in the 13th century and Henry of Winchester — better known as Henry III — spent much of his time in the city during a period when an early form of representation was emerging.

It has to be admitted that the citizens of Winchester, like many elsewhere, did not distinguish themselves at the birth of democracy. In 1264 they were given the chance to aid one of the prime advocates of parliamentary government, the younger Simon of Montfort, but they chose otherwise.

The monks were in favour of the new man (for reasons given below) and tried to control the King's Gate beside the main entrance to the Cathedral Close to welcome him and his army to the city. But the townsfolk got wind of events and swarmed down St Swithun's Street.

Fighting broke out and several monks were killed, according to some accounts. No doubt the abbot and his community were grateful for the protection of the close wall, which was built in the 1150s and still stands. However, the townsfolk caused considerable damage by starting a fire which destroyed the close gate and Kings's Gate. The existing gates in this part of the city and the beautiful little church of St Swithun-upon-Kingsgate were built to replace the earlier structures.

In the following year Simon of Montfort did eventually enter the city and provoked a good deal of street fighting. However, the medieval castle remained impregnable and the 'champion of representation' had to retire without taking Winchester.

In the same year Henry III and his son Prince Edward were taken prisoner at Lewes in a critical phase of what is called the Baron's War.

The Great Hall as a courtroom, shown with the layout used for an IRA bomb trial held in 1973
(Courtesy of the Chief Constable of Hampshire)

For Due Celebration of William of Wykeham

'To anyone who tries to trace the activities of Wykeham through the documents, he give the impression of having led the life of an indefatigable man of business.'

— Peter Partner

A man of humble birth who can make a fortune, found a great school, transform a cathedral into one of the finest in the world, hold the post of Chancellor of England and survive a charge of embezzlement must have some special qualities.

Yet William of Wykeham, the bishop who did all these things, has been described by a respected Winchester historian as having 'no genius or originality about him'. There are other aspects of this great man's life which seem to be puzzling, not least that he became Bishop of Winchester only a few years after taking holy orders relatively late in life. However, this is explicable in terms of the role of the medieval prelate, who was deeply involved in 'business'. Thus William was able to leapfrog the church hierarchy on the basis of his experience as an architect, surveyor, administrator and accountant.

He started life as William Long, born into a peasant family in the Hampshire village of Wickham, near Fareham. His intellect was clearly outstanding for at an early age he was sent to Winchester to further his education at the priory grammar school, which stood near the west end of the cathedral.

He was also helped by the patronage of the High Sheriff of Hampshire, Sir John Scures, who was appointed Constable of Winchester Castle and took William as a young boy of fourteen years of age to be his secretary.

The bishop of the time, William of Edyngton, also spotted his talents and introduced him to Edward III when he was in Winchester. Then followed twenty years of professional work during which he rose from being Clerk of the King's Works at Windsor to Chief Surveyor of the Royal Castles and Warden of Forests and Woods.

As he rose in rank he made a personal fortune. One of the towers be built at Windsor is said to bear the ambiguous inscription (in Latin): 'This made Wykeham'!

When William was appointed Bishop of Winchester in 1366 he not only took on a lucrative position but came to it as a self-made man of means. His church career was not, however, without its financial problems, for in 1376, five years after a stint as Chancellor, he was accused of embezzling public funds.

Towards the end of his life he financed a new form of independant educational foundation for poor, bright boys. The result was Winchester College, founded in 1382 and opened in 1394, which provided a model of Public School education. In modern times many of its pupils have followed distinguished careers in government and business, though William of Wykeham's original idea was to prepare boys for a life in the church.

Winchester College was set up as a feeder school for New College, Oxford, which William of Wykeham had already founded. The charter provided for a warden and ten fellows, two masters, seventy scholars and a staff of chaplains, choristers and chapel clerks. They were to live 'college-wise and study grammar' in the buildings which William of Wykeham built outside the city wall on what is now College Street.

Originally the college was ranged around two courts, still standing, which contained the Warden's Lodgings, Chapel, Hall, School and a variety of ancillary buildings such as the brewhouse. The college still has most of its original buildings but has now spread to cover a large area of south-east Winchester between St Cross Road and the river.

The foundation always allowed 'commoners' (non-scholars) to attend the college, but the practice of taking additional pupils gained momentum in the last century, when masters set up their own, self-contained houses in the neighbourhood and ran them like mini-businesses.

Today Winchester College offers a very wide choice of subjects, but until the present century its curriculum was extremely narrow and consisted of an unrelentless diet of the Classics. Mathematics has also been taught for a long while, but such subjects as English, modern languages and science were not taken seriously until relatively recently.

The idea of an independant scholastic foundation like Winchester College was copied some fifty years after its inception, when Eton College and its twin foundation, King's College, Cambridge, were set up. Not only were the details of the foundation as drawn up by William of Wykeham closely followed, but the Winchester headmaster, William Waynflete, was commandeered and cartloads of soil were carried from the college grounds to the site of the new school in Windsor!

The other major work which William of Wykeham paid for out of his own resources was the remodelling of the interior of the cathedral. The towering fluted columns of the nave were his inspiration. He set

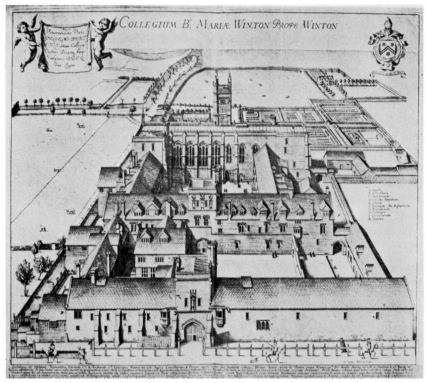

Winchester College in 1675, virtually unchanged from its original form

out to transform the gaunt Norman interior to a thing of beauty (compare the north and south transepts, which are in the original style) by recarving the original round plain pillars and inserting a 'false ceiling' of fine-ribbed vaulting.

His plans followed earlier attempts to beautify the cathedral by his predecessor Bishop Edyngton, who took down the twin towers that once adorned its west end and reduced its length by forty feet to give the present West Front. The squat windows at the west end of the north aisle are also Edyngton's work. To these William of Wykeham added the taller, more elegant windows which now pierce the length of the cathedral on both sides.

Recarving the Norman stonework proved to be very time-consuming and after the first eight pillars at the west end had been refashioned a new strategy was adopted. Thereafter, the nave was transformed by cladding the slimmed-down pillars with masonry carved 'in the workshop'.

William, who was 70 years of age when the work began, also made provision for his own burial by incorporating a chantry chapel into the south aisle. His effigy, attended by three diminutive monks, can still be seen. It stands at the spot where he is said, as a young boy, to have listened to mass.

The cathedral nave, started by William of Wykeham but not finished until long after his death (Courtesy of John Crook)

He died in 1404 at the episcopal palace at Bishop's Waltham, to the south of Winchester, only a few miles from his birthplace. The ruins of this country residence of the Bishops of Winchester, one of several in the diocese (there were others at Merdon, near Hursley, and at Marwell) can still be seen.

The Round Table and the Birth of Young Arthur

For many a petty king ere Arthur came
Ruled in this isle, and ever waging war
Each upon other, wasted all the land...

— Tennyson

Although the legends of King Arthur rallying the British against Saxon invaders have rarely been taken literally they were once important because they looked back to a time when British soil was held by its 'true' owners.

In particular, they predated the Christian missions of Augustine and Birinus and hence the rule of Rome.

Henry VIII was one of many who sought to remind foreigners of this fact and in particular Charles V, the Holy Roman Emperor, who in 1522 came to the Great Hall of Winchester Castle to see the Round Table which still hangs there. At this time British kings claimed to trace their lineage via Arthur to Constantine the Great, the first Christian Roman emperor.

Henry VII also made use of this romantic association between Winchester and King Arthur when in 1486 he brought his wife, Elizabeth of York, to the city to await the birth of their first child, Arthur.

His birth and the presence of royalty in the city were a source of great delight to the 'pomp-starved' citizens of Winchester who celebrated wildly. Pipes of wine were set up in the Cathedral Yard. The cathedral was elaborately adorned and lighted with torches. A procession of the 'great and the good' followed the couple and their child to the black marble font, which had last been used to christen a royal child in the case of Henry III.

Although Prince Arthur died in his teens and did not therefore succeed to the throne, his brother Henry, like his father, also looked on the ancient British king as an ancestor and used this assumed lineage to upstage the Holy Roman Emperor during his visit to the city.

Undoubtedly many of the visitors who over the years came to the Great Hall to see the Round Table on its west wall (before 1873 it was at the opposite end) may have half-believed the alleged connection with Arthur;

44

and truth to tell, even the experts knew little of the history of the table until relatively recently.

Ten years ago a piece of careful historical detective work carried out by Professor Martin Biddle and his colleagues revealed many of the secrets of this relic. The researchers did not seriously believe that it dated from the legendary age of Arthur, yet 'no one knew how old it was, whether it had ever been a table, or why it had been made and eventually hung up to become the great symbol now known across the world'.

When the table was taken down it was soon discovered that it had, indeed, been a table — with twelve legs around the periphery and supported centrally with a great leg. This huge piece of timber was secured by means of jointing similar to that employed by the millwright 'to clasp the axle of a mill-wheel'; it is the oldest known example.

The age of the timber was determined by taking samples from the 51 wedge-shaped planks which make up the surface of the table. Matching tree-rings with known patterns of growth and techniques of radio-carbon dating both came up with similar answers, suggesting that the relic had been made in the 13th century, towards the end of the reign of Henry III or early in the reign of Edward I.

The experts plumped for Edward I, who once swore on oath that he would construct a table like King Arthur's and was present in 1286 at Glastonbury at the opening of the tombs believed to be those of Arthur and his wife, Guinevere.

The chivalrous picture on the Round Table dates from the late 18th century but it is an exact overpainting of the original made for Henry VIII to impress visitors. The face of 'Arthur', who sits in state at the top of the picture, was modelled on that of Henry VIII himself. Painted around the edge are the names of the twenty-four knights who served him — 'Sir Launcelt, Sir Galahallt, Sir Bedivere' and the rest.

The Arthurian legend is mentioned in early English and Welsh chronicles but it was really medieval French authors who devised the traditional cycle of legends. According to these Arthur asked for a 'portable' round table to be made to seat a large number of knights — one version gives a figure of no less than sixteen hundred men!

The legend maintains that King Arthur is slumbering 'until called to arms once more', though he is allowed once every seven years to make an appearance. One of the places where he is said to have been sighted is in Winchester, on the appropriately named Sleeper's Hill, which is on the western outskirts of the city.

At this very spot Bishop Peter des Roches, the 'evil genius' of Henry III, is said to have come upon King Arthur during one of his 'seven-year itches'. To prove that this incredible event actually took place, he granted the bishop an extraordinary power over butterflies: whenever

The carpentry of the Round Table, revealed during renovation of the Great Hall in 1976
(Courtesy of the *Hampshire Chronicle*)

he opened his hand one of these beautiful creatures flew up.

One of the most popular versions of the Arthurian legend taken from the French is Sir Thomas Malory's *Morte d'Arthur*, the earliest copy of which was once owned by Winchester College. It was recognised in the school library in 1934 by Walter (later Sir Walter) Oakeshott, who later became headmaster of the college and cathedral librarian. The manuscript was sold ten years ago to provide funds for continuing to finance attendance at the college of bright pupils from Hampshire Comprehensive Schools, following a change in Government policy.

None so Sure as a Winchester Catholic

'Having reported the persecution carried on by Catholics against Protestants... it is necessary, for the truth of history, to say something of that which the latter raised against the former...'
— John Milner, 1798

The religious turmoil of Tudor England was probably felt more keenly in Winchester than in any other city. Yet the establishment of the Church of England by Henry VIII and his destruction of the fabric of monastic England were generally welcomed locally.

This is perhaps surprising since the city had grown up as a major religious centre and had once had as many churches as you will now find shops! However, when Henry sent in his asset-strippers to dismantle the old order the glories of medieval Winchester were long dead and the city was run-down and poor. Many townsmen no doubt felt that the monasteries were 'enormous husks housing insignificant kernels'.

Of all the major monastic and charitable institutions which stood before the Reformation, only the cathedral, Winchester College and the hospitals of St Cross and St John survived physically. The Abbey of St. Mary's, which local people had in vain tried to retain, and Hyde Abbey, together with all the friaries, were suppressed and most of their buildings were torn down.

One other institution which was dissolved but survived physically was the ancient manor of Godbegot, a remnant of which still stands in the High Street, opposite the Old Guildhall. Willed to St Swithun's Priory by the widow of King Canute before the Norman Conquest, it was endowed with a special status which had long upset city burgesses. It held its own courts and its occupants were therefore immune from the jurisdiction of the city authorities, who responded by forbidding all trade between God-begotters and citizens and charging the former a large fee for the freedom of the city!

St Swithun's Priory was suppressed but many of its members made a relatively smooth transition to the new form of governing body which still administers the cathedral, the Dean and Chapter. The prior became the first dean, his Lodgings, which still stand, became the Deanery, while the Refectory, which has gone, became the Common Hall. But in many ways it was a case of 'business as usual' in the Cathedral Close.

The priory did, however, pay a large cash sum to the king's agents

The Prior's Hall in the Cathedral Close became the Deanery after the Roman Catholic Priory of St Swithun was suppressed at the Reformation

and lost some of its more 'idolatrous' adornments, notably the celebrated shrine of St Swithun. This was dismantled in the dead of night by the king's appointed officers, aided by the Mayor of Winchester and some other townsmen. Records show that plundering the cathedral gained the Treasury about a thousand ounces of gold and many other valuables, including the bishop's mitre.

By reason of its position as a scholastic institution, Winchester College rode the storm, together with Eton and the Universities of Oxford and Cambridge. Indeed the college ultimately benefited by absorbing friary lands nearby, together with the College of St Elizabeth, an older chantry foundation set up to offer prayers, particularly for royalty and the bishops.

The Bishop of Winchester at the time was Stephen Gardiner, a man who played a prominent part in the later 'toings and froings' of the religious tide. He supported Henry VIII's actions to free England from the pope's authority but he was a convinced Catholic and could not stomach the rampant Protestantism of Cranmer and others. An example of the way in which the reforming zeal of the day interfered with church life was the edict that said that Winchester choristers had to grow long hair!

'Gardiner was deprived of his bishopric and imprisoned during the reign of Edward VI, only to be restored late when Mary Tudor came to the throne. Indeed, he officiated at her marriage in the cathedral to Philip of Spain, one of the grandest occasions to be staged in Tudor

Although the cathedral was, of course, saved from destruction it was left in a poor state of repair with no Dean and Chapter to care for it. These offices, together with the bishopric, had been abolished by the Puritans. A collection in the city did little more than provide enough funds to repair the roof and it was some years before political changes made it possible to restore the interior.

Local parish churches also suffered at the time. The little church of St Swithun-upon-Kingsgate, for example, was let to a man who kept pigs at one end and lived at the other. Similarly, St Lawrence, which stands near the City Cross on the site of chapel of the Norman Royal Palace, was also taken over. It served as a schoolroom and its stones were used for paving.

Clerics who refused to acknowledge the religious views of the Cromwellians were treated harshly. It is said that the Rector of Chilcomb, on the outskirts of Winchester, was reduced to walking the streets of London looking for scraps to eat.

Winchester after the Civil War was a place of defeat. Not only had it witnessed its own fall after the six-day siege of the castle by Cromwell and his troops in 1645, but there were other scenes of defeat nearby which were long remembered.

After taking Winchester the Parliamentarians turned north to reduce Basing House, the home of John Paulet, Marquis of Winchester and the greatest Royalist stronghold in Hampshire. And in the previous year the Royalists had been routed at the Battle of Cheriton, six miles to the east.

Two years after the fall of Winchester poor Charles I spent a night in the castle on that famous journey from Carisbrooke Castle to his execution in London. The mayor and aldermen, as was the custom, met him with the city keys but retired after being rudely reminded by the colonel of the guard that addressing the king had become an act of treason.

After the death of Oliver Cromwell his son Richard, who lived at Hursley, near Winchester, reigned for a short while but was obliged to flee abroad at the Restoration. After many years he returned to England, living in Middlesex under an assumed name, but after his death in 1712 he was buried at Hursley, where his descendants continued to live. Between his estate and the city lay the elevated site from which his father's troops had advanced, now the suburb called Oliver's Battery.

'Nelly' and Winchester's Restoration

'I must go and hear little Ken tell me of my faults'

— King Charles II

In the summer of 1684 a specially chartered coach made its way to the Winchester Races on the downs to deliver up the city's charter to the king, Charles II.

It was the culmination of two years of bitter infighting within the corporation between those who were willing to surrender the city to the Crown and others with Whiggish views who were outraged at the idea.

The ultimate decision was made by men who were dazzled by the promise of Royal Winchester and the opportunity to raise the city from a state of provincial decay to one of wealth and elegance.

Their hopes were well-founded since the old castle site had been given to the king and the building of a vast new palace was underway. Designed by Sir Christopher Wren and inspired by the palace of Versailles it was to be the king's principal country seat.

It was to be a huge E-shaped building with its courtyards facing towards the city and Cathedral Close with a total of one hundred and fifty rooms, including state apartments for the royal family and the king's mistress. Above a fine portico with marble columns was to be a lofty domed cupola taken to such a height that the king and his companions could view the fleet at Spithead.

The grand edifice, which would have dominated Winchester, was to have been linked with the west end of the cathedral by a series of seventy-seven steps and a grand avenue. Two hundred feet wide and 'lined with the houses of the nobility' it would have reduced the cathedral to a 'mere appendage' of the palace, later critics claimed.

The King's House, as the palace was called, was to be provided with a huge park to the west and south with a total circumference of ten miles. And all this was required in a great hurry by a middle-aged man of indifferent health.

Wren and his builders proceeded apace and within two years had

The King's House from the east as it might have been if completed, together with impressions of the castle from west and east. From Milner's History *of 1798*
(Courtesy of the Hampshire County Library)

completed the shell and roof of the vast palace. Then disaster struck: the king died and the grandiose scheme came to an end. Thereafter, the palace was pressed into use as a prison and for a variety of military purposes. One visitor in 1782 called it 'a miserable deserted intention of royalty'! In 1894 it was destroyed by fire and new barracks that retained a few faint features of Wren's design were built. From that time until 1985 they served as a major Army centre, most recently for the Royal Green Jackets, whose military museum is still there. The brigade now occupies a purpose-built camp on Flower Down, to the north of the city.

The hopes of those men who surrendered the city's charter at the Winchester Races in 1684 were therefore not realised, but the marks of the few years of glory that came during the Restoration period can still be seen. In fact, the sudden decision of the king to desert the turf of Newmarket for the Hampshire downs was only the ultimate bonus for a city that had gained considerably from a revival of the life of its Cathedral Close.

One of the key figures in this was Bishop George Morley, who was responsible for restoring the cathedral interior and also ordered the building of a grand new episcopal palace beside the ruins of Wolvesey. Started the year after the King's House, this was designed by Sir Thomas Fitch but was not completed finally until 1715. Today, only the west wing remains; it once more became the bishop's official residence in 1928.

There were also many other changes to the fabric of the close made after the Restoration (see p. 57). During his time as dean Dr William Clarke (1666-79) added a prominent brick extension to the east end of the deanery. Called the Long Gallery, it later served as an audience hall for Charles II when the Court was at Winchester.

In the Prior's Hall in the Deanery hangs a mirror which is traditionally said to have been used by the king's favourite mistress, Nell Gwyn, whose presence in the close was a cause of some discomfort to the cathedral canons. The bishop's chaplain, a Wykehamist called Thomas Ken, is said to have refused to allow her accommodation (see p. xx). When appointing Ken to the bishopric of Bath and Wells, Charles II is reputed to have remarked: 'Who shall have it but that ugly little man who would not give poor Nelly a lodging!' (see p. 59).

One other haunt of the king and his mistress was Avington House, a few miles to the east of Winchester, beside the River Itchen. A later, elegant mansion still stands there in a superb lakeside setting, surrounded by some of the finest country in Hampshire.

The streets of Winchester are still adorned with some of the houses that were built or restyled to house the companions of the king when he came to the city. His brother the Duke of York resided in a fine house which still stands in St Swithun's Street where it meets St. Thomas Street.

His queen, Catherine of Braganza, stayed some distance from the close in the house on the southeast corner of the intersection of Canon Street with Southgate Street, while the lady who vied with Nell for his attentions, the Duchess of Portsmouth, lived at No. 4 St Peter Street. And the son of his father's favourite, the Duke of Buckingham, resided at 8/9 Kingsgate Street.

There are also other relics of this period, including a portrait of Charles II by Sir Peter Lely, which was presented to the city in 1683 and now hangs in the Guildhall. And on the high altar of the cathedral are a bible and book of common prayer which the merry monarch gave to the Dean and Chapter.

Behind Close Doors

'The life of a prebendary is a pretty easy way of dawdling away one's time; praying, walking, visiting — and as little study as your heart would wish.'

— Edmund Pyle

These delightfully frank lines were written during the first year of his office by a holder of Winchester prebend, i.e. the living given to a member of the governing body of the cathedral, the Dean and Chapter. Like all his colleagues, Edmund Pyle had a house within the close and was obliged by the statues of the cathedral to spend a certain minimum time living there.

This requirement sometimes led to trouble, as in the case of Dr Thomas Gumble, a man who was chaplain to the Army commander, General Monk, at the time of the Restoration. This was at a time when many clerics considered themselves fortunate to have survived Cromwell's rule and to be participating in 'the return of the church' to Winchester.

During the Commonwealth the Dean and Chapter were banished from the close and its houses were assigned to Parliamentary supporters. Only five of the twelve houses needed to accommodate the canons survived the period (and only seven of the canons themselves!), and two of these were partly demolished. Thomas Gumble was fortunate to be allocated one of the houses which were unscathed, No. 2 (now demolished), but duties in London kept him from the close for more than a decade.

The shortage of canonry housing at this time led to a bloom of new building, including the four brick houses in Dome Alley and the fine stone house to the west of the deanery, now used as diocesan offices. In fact, senior prebendaries became jealous of the smarter accommodation of their younger colleagues, since the cathedral statutes laid down that a canon of a particular rank had to occupy a given house. After 1670 this was changed, so that the senior men had first pick of a vacant house, which often led to a chain of house-moving!

Dr Gumble was not, however, concerned by the fact that his house was one of those in worst repair because it provided a good excuse for his failure to live there. He even refused access to workmen and managed

The Deanery: its three-arched porch dates from the 13th century

to be as disagreeable as possible. When he did finally decide to move in he added a curious three-storey extension to the house without asking the permission of the Chapter, which led to a strong rebuke from the bishop of the day, George Morley, who told him 'to be more careful in the government of his tongue and pen'.

The problem of 'Dr Grumble', who nonetheless was called by some 'an amiable and kindly man', was soon overtaken by his death and his house then became the home of a man of a very different sort, Thomas Ken (see pp. 56 and 88). He will inevitably always be remembered for refusing to allow Charles II's mistress Nell Gwyn to live at No. 2 The Close but his life is memorable for many other reasons. He wrote some famous hymns and two years before he left Winchester in 1685 went on a government mission to Tangier, with Samuel Pepys, who spoke well of his preaching technique but described the content as 'forced meat'.

Nell Gwyn was in fact accommodated in the close in a small brick extension that was added to the south end of the 15th century prior's hall that still stands to the west of the fine medieval arched porch of the deanery. Her lodging was demolished at the beginning of the last century. About fifty years later No. 2 was demolished, not because it was particularly ugly — in fact, it attracted artists — but because the close then had a surplus of houses.

This was due to the Cathedrals Act of 1840, which 'reformed' the Chapter by reducing the number of prebendaries from twelve to five. (In 1930 the number was reduced again, to four). The house called No. 4, which may once have been the priory infirmary, also became redundant and was used during the late 19th century by the Cathedral Choir School. It is now used as lodgings for the judges of the Western Circuit during the Assizes. Perhaps the lawyers sleep the better for knowing that, like an Oxbridge college, the close is locked each night.

One other house affected by the reduced need for canonry housing was No. 3, which in 1931 became the home of the newly founded Pilgrims School, a very musical prep school for choristers from the cathedral and 'quiristers' from Winchester College. The building incorporates substantial medieval remains, said to be those of a guest-house for pilgrims visiting the shrine of St Swithun (see p. 32). Its fine Pilgrims Hall dates from 1290 and has the oldest known example of a 'hammer-beam' roof in the country.

One of the former occupants of No. 3 was Dr John Nicholas, Warden of Winchester College before being appointed to a prebend in 1684. He grew rich and spent some of his money on an existing college building called 'School' and also glorified his own house in the close with fine oak panelling by one of Wren's master craftsmen.

Called 'wainscoting', this interior cladding added greatly to the comfort of old houses and was bought by incoming occupants, rather like fitted carpets are today. Much that is known about the close and its occupants comes from the meticulous research of John Crook, who has studied a surviving book which recorded these transactions and other matters.

To the west of the main buildings of Pilgrims School are the former deanery stables which abut the fine timbered facade of Cheyney Court.

ı nıs was once the seat of the bishop's power in Winchester, for a large part of the city was under his jurisdiction and subject to his courts held in this building. Until the reform of local government in 1835 he had judicial powers in the cathedral precinct and a large part of the city outside the walls.

Alongside Cheyney Court is the main entrance to the close from St Swithun's Street. There are also entrances for pedestrians at the south-west corner of the cathedral and alongside the surviving arches of the Chapter House, where a tunnel called the Slype provides a short-cut to Colebrook Street. It passes No. 1. The Close, a handsome brick house which dates largely from 1727, but includes a wing of an earlier building of 1699.

This house is traditionally the home of the Canon of the 1st Prebend and is now occupied by the suffragan Bishop of Basingstoke. When the Diocese of Winchester included much of Surrey it was here that the suffragan Bishop of Guildford lived (while the Bishop of Winchester himself often lived at Farnham Castle!). One of the best-known holders of this office was George Sumner, whose wife Mary founded the Mothers' Union.

Although the first meeting of this club for young mothers was held in 1876, at Old Alresford, where George Sumner was rector, it was whilst living at No. 1 The Close that his formidable wife built up a modest idea into an international organisation.

Pilgrims School, with the late 13th century Pilgrims' Hall on the left

Izaak Walton and River Talk

'I am not of a cruel nature; I love to kill nothing but fish'

— *The Compleat Angler*

It is quite easy to visit Winchester without realising that it was founded beside the River Itchen, one of the best-known chalk streams in the world. This is because the main thread of the river to the east is entirely outside the area of the old walled city and water is carried within by a complex system of small brooks.

These smaller streams have an ancient origin and are thought to have been laid out as mill-leats in the 9th century, at the same time as the grid pattern of the city's street. The modern names Upper, Middle and Lower Brook Streets reveal former streams that have now been culverted.

Throughout the Middle Ages the water of the Itchen served Winchester's many mills, most of which were owned by the bishop. Abbey Gardens in the centre of the city is now skirted by the charming stream which once powered the mill of St Mary's Abbey, while the City Mill below St Giles's Hill, now owned by the National Trust, was turned by the main river, which lower down is called the Weirs.

Mills were used to grind corn but also for other purposes, notably 'fulling' or bulking-out cloth, a process which was once carried out by treading the cloth barefoot. Clothmaking was an extremely important industry in Winchester during the Middle Ages and its many processes made good use of the plentiful local supply of water.

Today the river is seen to best advantage as it runs from City Bridge around the old walls to Wolvesey, or further south in the water meadows between Winchester College and St Cross Hospital. Although the river was undoubtedly made navigable in the late 17th century, there is also a strong tradition that in the Middle Ages it was open between Southampton and Winchester and beyond to Alresford. Modern studies suggest, however, that almost all goods from the coast came by cart, including stone for such major buildings as the castle and cathedral.

It is a measure of the value of the river as a source of power in the Middle Ages that the mills were never bypassed in favour of a canal.

Dome Alley, where Izaak Walton lived with his daughter and son-in-law until the end of his life. (Courtesy of the Hampshire County Library)

When this was eventually achieved Winchester had declined so much as an urban centre that the new waterway never became profitable.

Another factor that had to be considered in making changes to the river was its fisheries, particularly for salmon. Nonetheless, most fish sold in the city came from the sea and it seems unlikely that Itchen trout and salmon ever played more than a minor role in Winchester's diet.

Today, the right to fish the river, whose banks are privately owned over most of its length, is much sought after by those who can afford it. It thus seems natural to those who visit the cathedral to find there the memorial window to Izaak Walton, author of *The Compleat Angler*, who in old age lived in the city. (Less easily seen is a statue of him at the top left-hand corner of the altar screen.) But the link between the famous river and the famous angler is rather tenuous.

Izaak Walton came to Winchester from Worcester after a successful business career in London, where he was a draper. He left the capital because of his strong Royalist cum Anglican sympathies at a time when the Puritans were supreme. The first, slim edition of *The Compleat Angler* was published in 1653, the year in which Cromwell became Lord Protector.

After the Restoration the celebrated angler became steward to the Bishop of Worcester, George Morley, and later came with him on his appointment to Winchester in 1662. By all accounts the two men were close friends and Izaak spent much time at Farnham Castle, which was then the principal palace of the bishop.

Izaak's attachment to the cathedral was cemented by a number of family relationships. He was enabled to live in the close through the marriage in about 1676 of his daughter to a canon, Dr William Hawkins. She was also the half-sister of the renowned hymn-writer Thomas Ken (p. 59), who was also a cathedral canon, so for a while they were all able to live in close proximity in Winchester.

Ken's house was demolished in the last century (see p. 58) but the house where Izaak spent his last years still stands to the west of the Deanery in Dome Alley, the last house on the right. When Izaak took up residence it was one of the newest houses in the close — it still is!

He no doubt spent some of his time walking the banks of the Itchen, though whether he fished it or not is unknown. It is interesting to note that *The Compleat Angler* was based more on other people's writings than first-hand experience. Its charm over the years (though surely few read it today) came from the manifest goodheartedness and cheer of the author and his delight in the countryside.

The following passage suggests that Itchen 'fishermen' then used methods that would bring a rush of blood to the head of a modern dry-fly angler:

Izaak Walton, author of The Compleat Angler

> And you are to know that in Hampshire, which I think exceeds all England for swift, shallow, clear, pleasant brooks, and store of Trouts, they used to catch Trouts in the night, by the light of a torch or straw, which, when they have discovered, they strike with a Trout-spear, or other ways.

Izaak had to admit, however, that when he witnessed these methods he did not like what he saw.

There is a tradition in the close that a summer house in the former garden of Thomas Ken's house was a haunt where Izaak and his friends — perhaps including Bishop Morley — collected. It is easy to imagine that he entertained them with angling talk, yet it is more likely that he spoke of the serious biographies of churchmen and men of letters that he wrote during his time at Winchester. Certainly the library used by Bishop Morley, which he bequeathed to the cathedral, did not contain a copy of his friend's renowned book.

The Itchen, and its sister stream the Test, obtained their reputations as prime sporting rivers during the last century when the coming of the railway made it possible for London-based men to spend the weekend in the country. All the controversies that fishermen relish have been fought on the banks of these rivers, paricularly that which followed the invention of the nymph (a form of sunk artificial fly) by G.E.M. Skues, who first fished the Winchester Itchen in 1893 and continued to do so for more than fifty years.

The Assizes and the Case of Alice Lisle

'. . .the terrible scene in Winchester Hall when the foul-mouthed judge raved and cursed, and the astounded Hampshire gentlemen would fain protect the aged prisoner but dare not, redounds to nobody's credit but the victim's.'

— D.H. Moutray Read

Although burning at the stake is generally thought of as a barbaric practice that died out several centuries ago, it did in fact continue in Winchester until the early years of the last century. There were two notorious cases tried at the Assizes, both of which involved the crime of 'petit treason', the murder of a husband by his wife.

In 1819 at Gallows Hill on the Andover road to the north of the city a Portsmouth woman was executed by burning for the murder of her husband. A similar event had taken place in 1784, when another woman was similarly executed, while her lover was hanged alongside her.

These terrible scenes, which drew huge crowds, were one of the many similar sensational events that mark the history of a city which has seen Assize Courts since their inception. Modern courts are held in the new buildings that adjoin the east wall of the Great Hall, though for centuries many famous legal trials were staged in the hall itself.

Here in 1603 Sir Walter Raleigh and others were found guilty of plotting to overthrow James I, though they were reprieved as the scaffolds were being put up on the Castle Green, the traditional place of execution in the city. It had been intended to hold the trial in London, where Raleigh met his end at the hands of the executioner 15 years later, but an outbreak of the plague drove the king and his court to Winchester. To accommodate the vast influx of people, Winchester College was taken over and its staff and pupils banished to the country.

In more recent years the Great Hall has seen the trials of the Price sisters and other IRA terrorists.

For a period between 1874 and 1938 Assize Courts were held in purpose-built premises to the east of the Great Hall, but settlement into the former ditch of the medieval castle made it necessary to return the proceedings 'temporarily' to the older venue. The judicial 'stage sets' inserted into Henry III's hall for so long could finally be cleared to reveal its full splendour when new Law Courts were opened alongside in 1974. These communicate with the Great Hall via a pair of fine stainless steel gates made to commemorate the wedding in 1981 of the Prince of Wales and Lady Diana Spencer.

During the 18th century, when Winchester was much favoured by Society, the dates of summer Assize Courts helped to mark the diary, along with the races and the theatre. Today most Wintonians are scarcely aware of the presence of the circuit judges, whose public ceremonials have in recent years been curtailed by security considerations.

One of the trials which most affected the locality was that in 1685 of Alice Lisle, the widow of Colonel John Lisle, who had close connections with Winchester. He was its M.P. and Recorder, and was also for a short while Master of St Cross. However, he was also a Parliamentarian in a Royalist city and this made him extremely unpopular. At the Restoration he was disgraced, the more so for being one of those who had signed Charles I's death warrant. He fled to Switzerland but was pursued there and in 1664 was murdered by 'three ruffians hired for the purpose'.

Interestingly, John Lisle's opposition to the Crown had its roots in a visit of the king to Winchester at a time when there was a bitter dispute between the corporation and the Dean and Chapter of the cathedral. It boiled down to the question of the rights of the city within the close. The conflict was underlined by such comic events as the mayor tripping over the legs of a cathedral dignitary at prayer and wearing his hat throughout services!

Throughout her long widowhood Alice Lisle, or 'Dame Alicia Lisle' as she was called by many, lived at Moyles Court, in the south-west of the county. She never forgot her husband's Parliamentarian passions and often gave shelter to non-conformists. Her downfall came after the Monmouth Rebellion of 1685, that unsuccessful attempt to oust the newly crowned James II. In the rout that followed the Battle of Sedgemoor the Duke of Monmouth fled and was found near Ringwood disguised as a shepherd. Two of his supporters sought shelter nearby at Moyles Court, where they were discovered by an ex-Cavalier with a strong personal grudge against John Lisle.

The upshot was that the elderly widow found herself at the Winchester Assizes accused of harbouring traitors in a court presided over by the notorious Judge Jeffreys. He lived up to his reputation for ruthlessness by bullying the jury until it provided the verdict he required. Although they were inclined to acquit the poor woman, they were sent back several times to reconsider their decision, and eventually declared her guilty of treason.

Some later commentators have been kinder to Jeffreys, suggesting that

'Alice Lisle concealing the fugitives', painted in 1857 by Edward Ward for the Palace of Westminster, where it still hangs in the corridor between Lords and Commons (Crown Copyright)

he established the truth in a 'masterly though brutal manner'. However, he was determined that Alice Lisle should be sentenced and executed without delay: he condemned her to be burnt at the stake forthwith.

To their credit, the Dean and Chapter and other prominent citizens immediately made an appeal to Jeffreys, who allowed time for the king to consider his mercy. As a consequence the sentence was 'reduced' from burning to beheading, which was carried out on the 2nd of September near a spot marked by a plaque on the wall of the City Museum. The loss of this elderly lady's life exposed for many the cruelty of James II's new reign and helped to spell the end of monarchic power.

Local opposition, however, did not prevent James II from visiting Winchester two weeks later, when he stayed with Bishop Mews, an exceedingly ugly military-minded churchman who despite his age had fought on the king's side at Sedgemoor. A portrait shows him wearing a large black patch on one cheek, which presumably covered an old battle wound.

Two years later the king was in the city once more, when the question of his religious bias was raised by Lord Churchill in the Deanery Gardens. James II is said to have replied: 'I will show favour to my Catholic subjects, and be a common father to all my Protestant subjects of what religion soever, but I am to remember that I am king, and I am to be obeyed.'

Just over a year later a country that could no longer bear such stuff and nonsense invited William of Orange to take power. Perhaps the execution of Alice Lisle had played some small part in these far-reaching changes.

Mayhem in College

'In 1830 the school was little different from its medieval self except that there was more accommodation for Commoners, more organised games, and fewer trappings of the religious life.'

— James Sabben-Clare

Any misconception that Winchester College has always been a civilised, untroubled society of learned gentlemen is readily dispelled by looking back into the records.

Understandably, tensions ran high at the Reformation when Protestant and Catholic came into open conflict. At Winchester the cause of the new religion was held by William Ford, who held the position of 'usher' and had a room close to the college chapel.

Like many Protestants he detested the statues and 'golden images' which cluttered the inside of the church and one night decided to pull them down. This he did by tying a length of cord from one to the other and then in the middle of the night pulling it tight from — as he thought — the safety of his room.

The almighty row awakened the whole college and masters and boys alike were astonished to see the destruction. As a contemporary account put it, 'all the golden godes came downe with *heyho Rombelo*'!

Although the end of the cord lay loose at the church door and Ford was found in his bed, he was the prime suspect and suffered at the hands of supporters of the 'old religion'. One night they laid in wait in the shadows of the King's Gate and set upon him with staves, leaving him for dead.

Both Ford and Winchester College survived these troubled times. But the ending of a semi-monastic religious function at the Reformation brought difficulties to the school that took three hundred years to sort out. It is hardly surprising that an institution rooted in the Middle Ages

Outer Gate, Winchester College, which dates from the original building of the late 14th century

Warden George Huntingford, who presided over a rebellious period in the college's history (Courtesy of the Warden and Scholars of Winchester College)

could not go through the nineteenth century without some change. Admittedly the impetus had to come from outside, from a Government commission set up to investigate the college, together with other Public Schools, in the 1860s.

An earlier commission of 1818 had almost undermined the status quo when it had suggested that the 'surplus' revenues of the college be used to support more scholars. But that idea had been rejected because it went against the original intention of the founder!

The Public School Act that eventually followed the later commission was typical of the reform that swept through the British institutions and it led to an ultimatum. Either the Warden and Fellows had to reconstitute the schools' government on the lines of the new legislation or a new set of men would be chosen for them. They chose to do nothing and thereby lost control to a variety of nominated men from the universities and other public bodies.

The fact is that for many many years the fellows, whose original function included a priestly role, lived off the revenues of the college and did virtually nothing in return. They had no teaching responsibilities and after the Reformation did not even live in the college.

The Warden, too, had the benefits of a lifelong sinecure that required the absolute minimum of effort and gave rich rewards. In the 17th century his allowance, in addition to free lodgings, included two whole sheep and 100 oysters each week and fifteen gallons of beer per day!

The life of the boys was in stark contrast. They had to rise at 5.30 a.m. but received no food or drink until several hours later, when a breakfast of bread and beer was served in primitive conditions. They slept on hard wooden bedsteads and were subjected to the callous brutality

Tea-time: the college rebellions were relatively recent history when scholars posed for this photograph (Courtesy of the Hampshire Country Library)

of senior boys and prefects. Indeed, one of the key features of the 'management policy' of its founder had been to employ a minimum of teachers. Thus in 1836 when the school had 150 boys there were only seven masters, compared with seventy for the present-day complement of 650 boys.

One other rule of school life was that boys were confined closely to school premises: College Street and Kingsgate Street alongside were very definitely out of bounds. It was the strict application of this rule that in 1793 led to a serious rebellion amongst the boys at a time when the spirit of the French Revolution was in the air.

It all started when a prefect slipped out to hear the Band of the Bucks Militia in the cathedral close. The Warden at the time was George Huntingford, a man who was later, perhaps unjustly, described as 'a lickspittle to the great and a bully to the young'. He decided to punish the prefect by depriving the whole school of its Easter leave.

Uproar! The senior boys joined forces and took over the school. They commandeered the keys from the porter and locked up the warden and two other men. The Red Cap of Liberty was raised to the top of the main gate and the boys prepared for a siege by loosening the stones of the parapet and taking up slabs of paving.

The warden was not, however, entirely incommunicado and managed to get a message to the High Sheriff of Hampshire, who came with a posse. He decided to use 'gently, gently' tactics and the rebellion fizzled out. But meanwhile Huntingford had written to the parents of the boys, insisting that they 'apologise or resign'. Feelings ran so high that they all chose to resign.

The sorry affair was in fact the last of four rebellions which took place during the headship of Joseph Warton, who was forced to resign himself. He was a colourful man who was said to be 'more at home in St James's coffee house than in a classroom trying to conceal his lack of accurate scholarship'. He belonged to Dr. Johnson's Literary Club and is credited with encouraging a pre-Romantics flush of poetry amongst Winchester pupils.

Another rebellion broke out under Huntingford's wardenship in 1818, when the headmaster of the day, Dr Gabell, tricked the boys into believing that they could escape home, only to run into the arms of the Army. He was never forgiven. As Canon Firth wrote in his history of the college: 'The young gentlemen of Old England could be ugly customers when driven to it, and meanness was to them the unforgivable offence.'

Although modern life at Winchester College is, by all accounts, much more civilised than at earlier times, like all institutions it can react violently to an external threat. This was demonstrated most recently when plans were unveiled in the 1970s to route the London-Southampton motorway across the hallowed meadows that lie between the college and St Catherine's Hill.

The setpiece battle that ensued between officials and local protesters at a Public Enquiry in July 1976 was given new spice by the sight of the then headmaster of Winchester College, John Thorn, and other members of the M3 Joint Action Group being thrown out for rowdyism.

Jane Austen and John Keats in Winchester

I have lost a treasure . . .she was the sun of my life, the gilder of every pleasure, the soother of every sorrow.'

— Cassandra Austen

In the north aisle of the cathedral is a plain stone slab which marks the grave of Jane Austen, one of the most famous authors in the English language. Yet the words carved on the memorial manage to give no hint of the literary genius whose novels quietly enshrined the lives of the Hampshire middle class she came from.

An apocryphal story tells how a puzzled cathedral verger asked to point out 'Miss Austen's grave' was heard to enquire: 'Is there anything particular about that lady?'

It was fifty years before any mention of her literary gifts were to be seen in the cathedral, when her biographer James Austen-Leigh placed a brass tablet on the wall near her grave. Financed from the profits of his account of her life, it modestly claimed that she was 'known to many by her writings'.

In 1900 a stained glass window in her memory was unveiled above her tomb. It was paid for by public subscription and incorporates a glass-artist's pun, for the name of the figure of St Augustine which it includes is often abbreviated to 'Austen'.

Winchester has undoubtedly profited from the 'literary shrine of Jane Austen' and the popularity of this part of the cathedral is an interesting modern example of how the custom of visiting saintly shrines might have grown up in the past.

However, Jane's connections with the city are slender and sad: she came here from her home at Chawton, near Alton, on a wet Saturday afternoon at the end of May, 1817, and in less than two months was dead. She had been declining in health for a long while and she came to Winchester to be close to a local physician, Dr Giles King Lyford. He came from a prominent local medical family and is remembered by a memorial in the south-west corner of St Lawrence-in-The-Square.

Medical detective work by the physician Sir Zachary Cope claims to

have shown that Jane was suffering from a disorder of the adrenal glands, Addison's Disease, though it was to be several years before the condition was known to the medical profession. Others have suggested that she was being slowly poisoned by metals from cosmetics.

During her stay in Winchester she lodged at No. 8 College Street, which still stands, close to the booksellers P. & G. Wells, and is now owned by the college. Here she was attended by Dr Lyford and nursed by her beloved sister Cassandra, but her health continued to fail.

She was obviously extremely weak but the vivacity which her friends and relatives all loved did not desert her. One St Swithun's Day, only three days before her death, she wrote an amusing poem called *Venta* after the Roman name of the city, in which she poked fun at the fashionable people who were then assembling in Winchester for the summer race season.

The idea behind the poem was that in pursuing pleasure the members of Winchester Society had forgotten the simple virtues of their patron 'wet weather' saint, who warned: 'Set off for your course, I'll pursue with my rain'!

Before Jane died she made arrangements for her funeral in the

An old photograph of Paternoster Row, now partly overbuilt by the car park of the Wessex Hotel,
showing to the right the entrance to Keat's Walk
(Courtesy of Winchester City Museums)

cathedral and was buried there on July 24th, 1817. The cathedral burial register gives the stark details but contains an error, for the recorded date is wrong by eight days, probably because it was entered some while after the event.

Only two years after Jane's death Winchester also became the home for a short while of another great literary figure, the young poet John Keats. He stayed here for two months at a time when he was tortured by the 'failure' of his publications and was trying to work out what to do with his life. Eighteen months later he succumbed to tuberculosis.

He came to the city from Shanklin, Isle of Wight, and travelled via Cowes and Southampton with his literary friend Charles Brown. He took lodgings in a house which has never been positively identified, though the best guess is that it was to the north-east of the cathedral on the site of the present car park of the Wessex Hotel.

At the time a street called Paternoster Row ran along this edge of the Cathedral Yard, parallel with Colebrook Street. An avenue of limes lined the northern edge of the yard and then turned sharply towards the west front of the church. The trees have now been felled, but for many years the path was called Keat's Walk after a regular 'constitutional' he described in his letters.

Followed unwittingly by many strollers today, it passed the cathedral, went through the close, through the King's Gate, down College Street and continued alongside the river to St Cross Hospital. Keats regularly took this route, returning to his lodgings before dinner, which was then a mid-afternoon meal. Regular exercise and a quiet life in Winchester were slowly improving his strength and enabling him to think about the future.

In letters he left some memorable descriptions of the city in the early 19th century, of side streets which, he said, were 'excessively maiden-like: the doorsteps always fresh from the flannel' and door knockers with an 'almost awful quietness about them'. He wrote: 'I never saw so quiet a collection of Lions' and Rams' heads.'

Whilst in Winchester he composed one of his best-known poems, *Ode to Autumn*, a serene product of a troubled time. The 'stubble plains' which inspired him may have been in the corn-growing, Hyde area of the city, according to Katharine Kenyon. She suggests also that he may have taken a special interest in Jane Austen's work and been prompted by a passage in *Persuasion*, which talks of autumn: 'That season of peculiar and inexhaustible influence on the mind of taste and tenderness, that season which has drawn from every poet worthy of being read, some attempt at description, or some lines of feeling.'

The quiet, shy, dying young man left Winchester feeling in his heart that he had failed, that he should admit that after all he would not make a success of his poetry, that he should settle down to a job as a hack in an 'elegant periodical works'. But he left with pleasant memories of the city and its downland air 'worth sixpence a pint'.

Where Trollope Ends and St Cross Begins

'A man who entertains in his mind any political doctrine, except as a means of improving the condition of his fellows, I regard as a political intriguer...'

— Anthony Trollope

To the south of Winchester College beside the Itchen stands the prominent church and almhouses of the Hospital of St Cross. The word 'hospital' is used in the old sense of a place of hospitality, a charitable institution. It still is a home for elderly men, yet this charming part of the Winchester scene is generally remembered for what would now be called a 'Press exposé' of the last century.

Its notoriety was first earned in the columns of *The Times* in the 1840s

The Beaufort Tower, St Cross Hospital, seen from the quadrangle

and was guaranteed a long life by the successful publication in 1855 of one of Anthony Trollope's earliest novels, *The Warden*, which was clearly inspired by the scandal of St Cross.

As interesting as the sordid circumstances of this story, which are given below, is the fact that the history of St Cross is littered with examples of embezzlement that make modern misdemeanours look like poaching sticky buns at a tea-party.

Moreover, these shocking affairs were conducted in an institution that had been expressly set up to attend to the needs of men who were 'feeble and so reduced in strength that they can scarcely, or not at all, support themselves'. These were the words (in Latin) used in the charter drawn up by Henry of Blois, the Winchester bishop who had the original idea in the 1130s.

The history of St Cross seemed to be a constant tug-of-war between those who thought that it had been set up as a convenient way of growing rich without any effort and others who remembered the spirit in which it had been founded.

Almost from the beginning there was a battle over who controlled it. Bishop Henry granted it to the Knights Hospitallers of St John in 1151 but during the next fifty years it bounced back and forth between the bishopric and the Knights, with quarrels between the Pope and the Crown as a side issue.

One legacy of the Knights is the silver Maltese cross and black gowns which mark the men who still live at St Cross under the foundation of Bishop Henry. This originally allowed for thirteen brethren and a daily meal for a hundred other poor men. It also laid down that the Wayfarer's Dole should be given to any traveller who asked for it, an offering still held out to anyone with the temerity to knock at the porter's lodge.

Even after settlement of the early quarrels over rights, which went in favour of the bishop, St Cross suffered from the appointment to its Mastership of men who often never came near the place. And when they did it was often merely to appropriate property or skim off revenues. Thus in the 1330s the Master, Peter of Galiciano, is said to have stolen the alms and misused the rents and profits of the hospital.

However, St Cross was soon blessed by the arrival of a new man who seems to have tried to improve the lot of the brethren and at the same time carried on with building the church, which was still unfinished. This was William of Edyngton, who later was appointed Bishop of Winchester. Then followed a period when the administrations of William of Wykeham (see p. 40) brought benefits, but not before an affair which would surely have moved Trollope to take up his pen with even more gusto.

Old photographs of the church of St Cross Hospital (above) *and a group of 'black brothers'* (Courtesy of the Hampshire County Library)

This concerned Sir Roger de Cloune, a Yorkshire rector who was appointed Master of St Cross and then proceeded to sell many of its assets and pull down its buildings. He also turned out the brethren in the belief that all he was obliged to do was to feed the poor outside the gates.

More amazingly, even when William of Wykeham had won a legal battle against the man, he clung on to his position in the hope (mistaken, as it happens) that he would be able to override the verdict by appealing to the Pope.

Under the patronage of William of Wykeham, who at one time included the Mastership amongst his many offices, the hospital prospered. However, the man whose charity enabled St Cross to be refounded and built more or less to its present form was another Bishop of Winchester, Henry Beaufort, a man whose normal instincts of intrigue and greed outshone those of any Master. In 1446 towards the end of his life he bought a new charter for St Cross from the Crown which ensured that it was more than adequately endowed for many years. At the same time he set up the Order of Noble Poverty (its brethren wear dark red gowns) to provide for thirty-five men and three women of noble birth who had fallen on hard times.

In fact it was many years before any new brethren were supported — and St Cross has never had a lady resident — though most of the buildings that can be seen today, including the fine tower at the entrance to the main quad, all resulted from Beaufort's foundation.

After surviving the changes of the Reformation, St Cross came under the mastership of Dr Abraham Markland in 1694, who decided to make good the loss of a written constitution. It included a phrase that was to cause all the trouble that gave Trollope his story, namely, that after the Master had provided for the brethren he could keep any surplus profits himself.

This provision was interpreted quite literally by a subsequent Master, Francis North, later styled Earl of Guilford, who was appointed by his bishop father in 1807. He grew rich on St Cross as well as a number of other 'livings'. Later estimates suggest that he pocketed between £50,000 and £250,000 from St Cross alone!

You might imagine that all this was done 'behind closed doors', but not so: in 1835 the Ecclesiastical Commissioners investigated Press reports of his affairs but decided, somewhat unhappily, that he was within his rights.

As mentioned above, he was later pursued by more Press reports but his downfall came nearly twenty years later when a clergyman who had retired to Winchester discovered some incriminating correspondence at St Cross during a spell as a locum chaplain. He had long wished to impugn the Earl and sent the letters to the Solicitor to the Treasury. However, it was five years before judgement was given against the Master, who resigned 'not really understanding what all the fuss was about', as Paul Cave puts it in his *History of the Hospital of St Cross.*

Today St Cross is, of course, fully reformed but it is still subject to the vagaries of financial pressures. Only two years ago the Charity Commissioners decided that to combat inflation the trustees could charge brethren for some of the costs of their 'sheltered accommodation'.

Survival of the Highest —
A Tale of Hospitals and Drains

'Winchester must surely be the only cathedral city to have a sewerage pumping station named after a dean.'

— Barbara Carpenter Turner

By a stroke of luck Winchester was the first place outside London to have what we would recognise as a hospital. Now called the Royal Hampshire County Hospital, it is this year celebrating its 250th anniversary by raising funds for a scanner. It was originally founded in a medieval building on the corner of Colebrook Street by a canon of the cathedral, Dr Alured Clarke. He came to Winchester in 1723 and lived in three different houses in the close, ending his days in No. 4, now the judges' lodging.

He had formerly been a royal chaplain in London and the blueprint for the new hospital was based on the example of St George's Hospital, Hyde Park. In October 1736, Dr Clarke, who himself suffered from a chronic painful illness, commemorated the opening of his new institution with a sermon in the cathedral.

One of the most impressive features of his foundation were the detailed rules laid down for its management. Accounts were examined weekly, bills paid promptly and daily 'visitors' toured the hospital to make sure that it was being properly run. Its apothecary was not only responsible for medicines but also had to draw up a diet sheet for each patient. Two surgeons attended daily and were obliged to finish their rounds by eleven o'clock each morning, though physicians only visited once a week.

It was what modern doctors might call an acute hospital; chronic or

Middle Brook Street, with the cathedral beyond, before the Brooks were culverted in the last century
(Courtesy of the Hampshire County Library)

infectious diseases were not treated and women 'heavy with child' were kept out. The idea, like today, was to limit treatment to those who could be cared for just as well at home. Patients were able to attend the hospital by subscribing in the same way as they might subscribe to a circulating library. It was therefore a form of private health care, though wards in the original plans labelled 'private' were intended for treating the sort of diseases that men and women in a garrison town are likely to give each other.

Twenty years later plans were made for a grander hospital to be built in Parchment Street, though the building once occupied in Colebrook Street survived until modern times. When it was demolished in 1959 beams bearing biblical texts were discovered: they can now be seen in the City Museum. In the early 18th century it must have been comforting

Dr Alured Clarke, founder of what has become the Royal Hampshire County Hospital (Courtesy of the Winchester Health Authority)

One of the beams recovered during demolition of the medieval building in Colebrook Street where Dr Clarke started his hospital in 1736 (Courtesy of Winchester City Museums)

for someone with venereal disease to glance up at the words: 'Despise not thou the chastening of the Almighty', or for a seriously ill patient to read: 'Like as the Father pitieth his children, so is the Lord merciful unto them that fear him'.

Despite the apparent advantages of a pioneering hospital, the general level of health in the city was poor during most of the last century, when the population expanded greatly (from 8,000 to 17,000 between 1821 and 1881). It was a time when the 'best part of town' was as likely to be favoured for its drains as for its view. Although the residents of the Cathedral Close and those able to live outside the city might enjoy reasonable health, the average Wintonian could only expect to live to the age of fifty, compared with the national average of fifty-eight.

This was one of the horrifying facts laid before a committee set up to investigate local drainage, following a petition signed in 1866 by all the doctors and surgeons in the city.

The gentlemen of the close had for centuries enjoyed a form of drainage. This was the Lockburn, a stream that came from the Abbey Mill and passed behind the east end of the cathedral through the lavatories of the priory. Another branch ran to the west side of the close, where other monastic buildings stood. Today these streams can still be heard running underground to join the watercourse that runs into the Itchen by the side of Winchester College.

According to tradition, the Lockburn was brought into the cathedral precinct during the 10th century by the reforming Saxon bishop,

The hospital purpose-built in Parchment Street in 1759, now demolished
(Courtesy of Winchester City Museums)

Aethelwold (see p. 15). He diverted the river 'a little above Abbot's Worthy', three miles to the north of the city, so that 'sweet floods of water abounding with fish' were directed to various parts of the city.

During the Middle Ages the Lockburn became severely congested, not only with sewage but with butchers' offal, which was tipped into any convenient watercourse. One of William of Wykeham's less celebrated acts was to arrange for a grille to be placed over the outlet to keep back the worst of the problem from his newly-founded seat of learning, Winchester College. At a much later date, drainage and health became major concerns at the college, particularly after an attack of typhoid led to the death of a boy in 1874.

The centre of the city in general also became an exceedingly foul place, particularly in the Brooks area, where open sewers also served as sources of drinking water. Life was much more pleasant on the West Hill, where water from wholesome wells was available and, after 1854, piped water. It was here, in the suburbs that grew up in the second half of the last century, that those who could afford to do so set up home.

Winchester finally solved its drainage problems in the late 1870s with a system that involved a pumping station in Garnier Road, situated between the playing fields of the college and St Cross. This was largely due to the efforts of a college housemaster, Frederick Morshead, who had served as mayor a few years earlier. The building with later extensions still stands. Since 1910 its pumps have been turned by steam raised from burning refuse.

The pumphouse took its name from Thomas Garnier, Dean of Winchester, who died in 1872 and is remembered as 'a man who fought injustice, bad housing, unemployment, poverty, a man identified with the solution of social problems'.

A strange twist in the sewage story of Winchester is that before the installation of a proper system one of its most notorious problems had come from its hospital in Parchment Street, which had a large cess-pit to the rear. Unfortunately, this was inadequate for the hospital's needs, which meant that sewage overflowed into Upper Brook Street.

Relief from this particular sewage problem came in 1868 when the hospital was moved to the lofty slopes of the West Hill, where it still stands. The design and layout of the new building were influenced by the advice of the Victorian nurse-heroine Florence Nightingale, who lived in Hampshire, near Romsey.

Below the hospital stands King Alfred's College, a college of higher education, originally founded in 1840 as the Diocesan Training College, which in 1862 had also moved up to the hill for health reasons, but soon found that the resited hospital's effluent brought a whole new series of problems. Drains were with good reason a recurring topic of conversation in Victorian Winchester!

The Royal County Hospital: modern medicine in a gothic building of 1868

The Diver who Shored-Up
the Cathedral

'Dear Sir, I have received a letter commanding me to be at Buckingham Palace... to receive the Royal Victorian Order... I would be grateful if you would inform me how to go on and anything I could do for the firm...'

— William Walker

One of the most unlikely memorials to be found in the cathedral is the bronze statue of a diver, William Walker, who is depicted in the traditional 'heavy boots and facemask' of his trade.

The story of how he laboured to underpin the great church has become the best remembered aspect of six years of vital work carried out during 1906-12 when the whole structure was found to be in danger of collapsing.

A massive repair programme not only secured the cathedral for future generations but also made William Walker one of Winchester's 20th-century folk-heroes. Daunting repairs have, in fact, been a constant feature of the life of the cathedral, because it is built in a hollow on peaty waterlogged ground. But the scale of the programme and its use of 'new technology' made it a subject of immense popular appeal.

During the early years of the century the annual reports of the architect of the day, John Colson, often referred to defects in the structure. In 1905 he invited the Dean and Chapter to give 'serious consideration' to signs of movement at the east end.

The south wall of the east end of the cathedral was leaning outwards to such a degree that its top overhung by more than four feet. The basic problem was that this part of the structure, which dates from the 13th century, had been built on a raft of logs laid down in a peat bog. It had never been very stable and soon after completion it had sunk at the east end, thereby 'breaking the back' of the cathedral.

The foundations of the cathedral were nowhere properly laid on firm ground, but the particularly deep beds of peat which overlie gravel under the east end made building in this area especially prone to sinking.

John Colson's report was referred to Thomas Jackson, a distinguished consulting architect, who dug a ten-foot ditch outside the south wall and discovered the remains of the original logs overlying the Itchen peat.

William Walker
(Courtesy of the Dean and Chapter of Winchester Cathedral and John Crook)

He, in turn, called in a consulting engineer, Francis Fox (incidently, a descendant of the 16th century bishop, Richard Fox), and together they made detailed plans for emergency works to shore up the structure and carry out work on other parts of the cathedral.

The news that the church was 'literally tottering on its foundations from end to end' was greeted nationally with great concern. One report concluded: 'The nation is not yet decadent enough to contemplate the loss of Winchester Cathedral.'

One of the complications of any 'deep repairs' to the cathedral is that the water table is not far below the surface. This is why the crypt, which lies beneath the east end, is regularly flooded and can only be visited in the summer months.

When the contractors started to dig beneath the cathedral to insert new foundations they found that removal of the peat layer allowed water to well up from the gravel beneath, making further work impossible. After much discussion it was suggested by Francis Fox that divers should be employed and within a month William Walker and another diver were on site.

They worked for the firm of Siebe, Gorman & Co, a large company which still flourishes and at the time employed more than two hundred divers. Walker was soon judged to be by far the better diver for the job and spent the next five years at work on the cathedral, working two four-hour shifts a day. He and his mate, William West, are estimated to have handled more than 25,000 bags of concrete during the underpinning operation.

This was done section by section. First a 'drift' was excavated under a part of the walls, almost to the level of the river gravel. This quickly filled with dirty water from the ground about, which had once been a graveyard. It was William Walker's unenviable job to descend into this murky hole to break through the final layer of peat and then to lay bags of concrete to seal the bottom of the drift. When these had set hard the hole was pumped out so that the foundations could be built up to the foot of the wall.

At the peak of the programme there were more than a hundred men involved, masterminded by the clerk of works, Edwin Long, whose surviving notebooks give a day-by-day record of the work.

The underpinning which Walker made possible was only part of a more extensive programme of works carried out at the time. The most obvious consequence of these are the ten flying buttresses which now line the south wall of the cathedral and give the support that was once provided by the cloisters of St Swithun's Priory. As inscriptions show, some of the buttresses were given as memorials — to Thomas Ken (see p. 59), to old Wykehamists, and to the well-known Victorian churchman

The flying buttresses built against the south wall of the cathedral during 1906-12 to make up structurally for the loss of the priory cloisters after the Reformation.

and Hursley rector, John Keble. Two others were also given by the Mothers' Union, which has its roots in the Diocese of Winchester (see p. 60).

At the same time the West Front was repaired and timbers and much of the leading of the cathedral roof were renewed. Two of the memorial tombs (chantries) for which Winchester is famous were also underpinned and repaired. They both stand behind the choir at the east end: that of Cardinal Beaufort, who refounded St Cross Hospital, is opposite William Walker's statue, while that of Bishop Waynflete, the first master of Eton and founder of Magdalen College, Oxford, is to the north and faces a statue of Joan of Arc.

Other works carried out to strengthen the structure included the injection of about five hundred tons of grouting into cracks in the stonework. Steel tie-rods were also inserted where necessary, some of which can be seen on the south side of the retrochoir close to Walker's statue. Today these rods enable engineers to check on the state of the structure, for any movement changes the tension in the rods and therefore the sound created when they are struck.

When John Colson made his original recommendations to the Dean and Chapter he suggested that it might cost about £3000. In fact, the total cost of all the work finally commissioned was £113,000 (perhaps two million pounds at current prices). The money was raised by a constant and energetic programme of fundraising carried out by Dean Furneaux and others. Completion of the programme of restoration in 1912 was marked by grand ceremonials, including a whole week of services. The main service was held on St Swithun's Day, July 15th, and was attended by King George V and Queen Mary and many other dignitaries.

The Honours List subsequently included the names of three of those involved in the work at Winchester: Jackson received a baronetcy, Fox a knighthood and Walker the Royal Victorian Order. But it is the memory of the diver that has endured. This was marked in March 1964 by the unveiling of the bronze statue referred to above. Sculpted by Sir Charles Wheeler, it was appropriately placed beside the Lady Chapel, above the foundations which Walker helped to underpin.

The diver himself did not live to witness the enduring interest shown in his work, for he died during the virulent influenza epidemic of 1918. He would no doubt have been rather puzzled.

Perhaps the most interesting question to ask about the Walker story is whether his work was merely a sensational happening seized upon by worried fundraisers or whether it was truly an extraordinary feat. The authors of a recent book, *The Winchester Diver*, have concluded that although Walker was undoubtedly a 'target for sightseers . . .he was also recognised as the essential figure . . .by the four experts involved in the preservation process'.

One of these, Francis Fox, was certainly in the best position to judge, for he was himself a qualified diver and often descended beneath the cathedral to inspect Walker's work.

Appendices

I. Winchester Words

The Castle: Site of the former Norman and medieval castles, now taken up by the Law Courts and the central offices of the Hampshire County Council

Cathedral The existing cathedral church built by the Normans in the 11th century. The Cathedral Close lies to the south and is enclosed by a wall. The surrounding land on the other three sides is called the Cathedral Yard

College of St Mary: The name given to Winchester College by its founder

Dean and Chapter: The governing body of the cathedral since the Reformation, when it took over from St Swithun's Priory (see below)

Diocese of Winchester: The bishop's domain once included much of Hampshire, Surrey and South London. With the exception of Portsmouth, which has its own diocese, it today only covers Hampshire and the Channel Islands.

Great Hall: The only standing building of the medieval castle to survive

Hyde Abbey: Originally founded as the New Minster by Alfred the Great and situated to the north of the cathedral. It moved in 1110 to land at Hyde, outside the North Gate of the city. It was suppressed at the Reformation

King Alfred's College: College of Higher Education, formerly the Diocesan Training College

King's Gate: One of two surviving gates of the walled city. It stands between the Cathedral Close and Winchester College

New Minster: The monastery founded beside the Old Minster and later moved to Hyde (see Hyde Abbey)

Nunnaminster: Nunnery founded by Alfred the Great's queen, Alswitha. It stood in the vicinity of the present Broadway and Abbey Gardens and was suppressed at the Reformation

Old Minster: The first cathedral church in Winchester, founded in the 7th century. Its outline is marked on the ground to the north of the present cathedral, which was built to replace it

Prebendary: The holder of a prebend, a living enjoyed by a member of the Cathedral Chapter

St Cross: District to south named after Hospital of St Cross, a charitable foundation of the 12th century

St Mary's Abbey: Another name for Nunnaminster (see above)

St Swithun's Priory: The former monastic community which served the cathedral church until the Reformation. Named after a former bishop and Catholic saint

Soke: Former area of the city governed by the bishop, now used to describe that part to the east of the river

'Toytime': Winchester College slang for 'evening prep', one of a large number of special words used at the school

Venta Belgarum: The name of the Roman city, meaning the market town of the Belgae, a British administrative area

West Gate: One of the two surviving gates of the walled city and now used as a small museum. It stands at the top of the High Street

Winchester College: The famous Public School for boys

Wintonian: An inhabitant of Winchester, from the Saxon name of the city, *Wintonceaster*

Wolvesey Palace (or Castle): The seat of the Bishop of Winchester, which lies to the south-east of the cathedral, though bishops for long periods ruled over their diocese from Farnham Castle

Wykehamist: A member of Winchester College, which was founded by William of Wykeham

II. Winchester: A Brief Chronology

(To the dates below must, of course, be added those of the great national events which influenced the whole country)

c.100-150 BC	Iron Age settlements in Oram's Arbour area and on St Catherine's Hill abandoned
AD 43	Roman conquest of Britain, leading to establishment of the walled town of *Venta Belgarum*, the fifth largest in Britain
c.350-400	Decline of Roman rule and of urban life in Winchester
495	According to the *Anglo-Saxon Chronicle*, the Saxons Cerdic and his son Cynric landed at a place that has been identified with Calshot, near Southampton, at the start of their campaign to take Wessex
662	Movement of bishopric from Dorchester-on-Thames to Winchester,

	a royal residence of the West Saxon kings, following their conversion to christianity by Birinus (635) and the building of the original Old Minster in 648
852-62	Bishop Swithun, later canonised
860	City attacked and laid waste by Vikings
871-99	Alfred, King of the West Saxons: rebuilt Winchester as a fortified urban centre
c.901	To north and east of Old Minster, respectively, New Minster and St Mary's Abbey founded by Edward the Elder, according to Alfred's will
963-84	Bishop Aethelwold: Old Minster expanded and rebuilt to accommodate St Swithun's shrine (971). Its community, the Priory of St Swithun, reformed according to the Benedictine Rule
1043	Edward the Confessor crowned in Winchester, though he was the first king to spend most of his time at Westminster.
1066	City surrendered to William the Conqueror, who was later crowned in the city (1068). Building of castle started
1079-93	Bishop Walkelin built the cathedral, and demolished the Old Minster
1086	Domesday Book compiled in Winchester, but later surveys covered the city itself (c.1110 and 1148)
1100	William Rufus buried in the cathedral after hunting accident (?) in New Forest. He granted the bishop the right to hold St Giles's Fair
1110	New Minster moved with Alfred's remains to Hyde
1129-71	Bishop Henry of Blois: founded St Cross Hospital (1136) and greatly extended Wolvesey Palace
1141	Siege of Winchester during civil wars of Stephen and Matilda
c.1180	Hereafter, the royal treasure kept in London
1207	Birth of Henry of Winchester, later Henry III
1222-35	Great Hall of the castle built, followed by many other changes, e.g. the West Gate rebuilt in 1240
1258	One of several Parliaments held in the Great Hall
1345-66	Bishop Edyngton: west end of cathedral rebuilt
1366-1404	Bishop William of Wykeham: founded New College, Oxford, and Winchester College (opened 1393)
1446	St Cross Hospital refounded by Cardinal Beaufort
1447-87	Bishop William Waynflete: headmaster of Winchester College (1429-42), founding head of Eton College (1443) and founder of Magdalen College, Oxford (1448)
1536-40	Reformation: Hyde Abbey, St Mary's Abbey and other foundations suppressed, including St Swithun's Priory. Cathedral now governed by Dean and Chapter

1554	Marriage of 'Bloody' Mary to Philip II of Spain in the cathedral
1603	Trial of Raleigh in Great Hall
1611	Speed's map of the city reveals a place shrunken within its own walls, with large areas of open space
1642	Castle taken by General Sir William Waller
1645	City taken finally by Oliver Cromwell's army. Charles I passed night in castle (1649), which was later destroyed
1660	Restoration: the bishopric is reinstituted and canons return to the Cathedral Close
1669-84	Thomas Ken prebendary at Winchester
c.1680	Baroque bishop's palace started at Wolvesey, though not completed until 1715
1682-85	Charles II and his court in the city. Building of King's House started (1682) but not finished
1683	Izaak Walton buried in cathedral
1685	Alice Lisle executed in the Square
1736	First hospital outside London founded by Dr Alured Clarke in Colebrook Street. Subsequently moved to Parchment Street (1759) and the West Hill (1868)
1778	*Hampshire Chronicle* moved to Winchester after being founded in Southampton six years earlier
1786	All but the west wing of the 17th century Wolvesey Palace demolished
1793	Serious rebellion of boys at Winchester College, the first of several
1817	Jane Austen buried in the cathedral
1819	John Keats lived in the city
1840	Number of cathedral canons reduced from twelve to five by statute. Founding of Diocesan Training College, which became King Alfred's College
1853	Earl of Guilford impugned by Chancery Court judgement that he was guilty of a 'wilful breach of trust' during his Mastership of St Cross Hospital
1876	Mothers' Union founded at Old Alresford, later centred on Winchester and Westminster
1878	Drainage scheme started with pumping station in Garnier Road
1888	Hampshire County Council set up by statute, with its offices at The Castle, Winchester
1906-12	Cathedral underpinned and repaired by efforts of William Walker the diver and others
1931	Pilgrims School founded
1968	Winchester Research Unit founded

1979   900th anniversary of the starting of the cathedral

1984   Oil discovered between Crawley and South Wonston on the outskirts
            of the city

1986   Domesday 900 Exhibition held in the Great Hall. Medieval Wolvesey
            Palace opened to public by English Heritage. New exhibition set up
            at Winchester Heritage Centre. Theatre Royal reopened after
            substantial refurbishment.

III. Further Reading

Biddle, M., *The Study of Winchester: Archaeology and History in a British Town*, 1984
— (ed.), *Winchester in the Early Middle Ages*, (Winchester Studies 1), 1976
— *Wolvesey: The Old Bishop's Palace, Winchester*, 1986
Biddle, M. and Beatrice Clayre, *Winchester Castle and the Great Hall*, 1983
Bussby, F., *Jane Austen in Winchester*, 1969
Bussby, F., *Winchester Cathedral: 1079-1979*, 1979
Carpenter Turner, B., *Winchester*, 1980
Crook, J., *The Wainscot Book: The Houses of Winchester Cathedral Close*,
    1984
Custance, R., (ed.), *Winchester College: Sixth-Centenary Essays*, 1982
Firth, J d'E., *Winchester College*, 1949
Green, M., *Winchester Cavalcade*, 1965
Henderson, I.T. and J. Crook, *The Winchester Diver: The Saving of a Great
    Cathedral*, 1984
Keene, D., *Survey of Medieval Winchester*, (Winchester Studies 2), 1985
Keynes, S. and M. Lapidge, *Alfred the Great: Asser's 'Life of King Alfred'
    and Other Contemporary Sources*, 1983
Kenyon, K.M.R., *Keats in Winchester*, 1947
Milner, J., *The History and Survey of the Antiquities of Winchester*, 1798
Rance, A., *Prospect of Winchester: A Guide to the City Museum*, 1978
Sabben-Clare, J., *Winchester College*, 1981
Vesey-Fitzgerald, B., *Winchester*, 1953
Woodland, W.L., *The Story of Winchester*, 1932

Index

(Page numbers for illustrations are in italics)